THE
LORD
OF THE
RINGS

THE
OFFICIAL STAGE
COMPANION

THE
OFFICIAL STAGE
COMPANION

Gary Russell

HarperCollins*Publishers*

CONTENTS

For years, I wondered how the vast scope of *The Lord of the Rings* might be realized theatrically, given the constraints of the live stage. Until Kevin Wallace and the creative team were able to develop the vision necessary to make a play that could truly live, it remained a dream. But now the dream is a reality. I am very proud to be associated with this inspiring production which so imaginatively and faithfully presents *The Lord of the Rings* on stage.

SAUL ZAENTZ

ACKNOWLEDGEMENTS

Before I raise the curtain and reveal exactly how and why *The Lord of the Rings* is in your theatre right now, there are a handful (well, a tankard-full actually) of people who I would like to introduce to you and to say thanks for all their help in making this book the fine object that it is:

First and foremost to Kevin Wallace, who let me into this world with such grace, good humour and honesty. To Rob Howell, Matthew Warchus, Shaun McKenna, Peter Darling, Christopher Nightingale, Simon Brindle, Rob Tannion, Alex Frith, Dave Brill, Carl Robertshaw and Irene Bohan, who tolerated microphones being pushed under their noses, emails out of the blue and my endless questions, but never once said no, even when they really had far better things to do.

To Andrzej Goulding, Megan Huish, Laurie Battle, Jane Thompson, Dirk Rueter, William Bennett and especially Melanie Southan, who aided and abetted me so kindly. To Chris Smith and David Brawn at HarperCollins for wanting this book to happen in the first place, and then asking me to do it. To Ian Farrington, who sat down and transcribed a majority of the interviews so quickly and efficiently.

Thank you one and all. And I sincerely believe that, given the chance, the audiences who are going to be spellbound for three hours each night will want to thank you with equal fervour.

INTRODUCTION

J.R.R. Tolkien's marvellous work of epic adventure (more formally known by its constituent parts as *The Fellowship of the Ring*, *The Two Towers* and *The Return of the King*) has been brought off the page before, in cartoons, on the radio and most notably in the Academy Award-winning movie trilogy, directed by Peter Jackson. But what producer Kevin Wallace, director/ writer Matthew Warchus and writer Shaun McKenna, along with their team of visionaries, have created on the stage is equally if not more spectacular an achievement. For, to take a story of more than 1,000 pages and successfully condense it into three hours of live performance, without losing any of the storytelling genius, any of the character and above all any of the charm, is nothing short of miraculous.

This book is presented as a celebration of that achievement, describing the genesis of the project, which has its unlikely beginnings in a circus tent in Germany, through to the eve of the stage experience.

But, as the following pages will explain, it's not been an easy road; it's been instead as long a journey as Frodo's, which for some members of the team stretches back over a decade. It's had false starts, fluid changes and farcical moments. But what has made it happen, what has allowed it to exist, is the fortitude, dedication and, above all, love for the project brought to it by everyone who has worked on it. A love not just for grand theatre, nor for presenting the best show possible, but a deep, unbridled passion for the craft of theatre, for developing and experimenting with proscenium staging and for giving the audience a night to remember. And, just when you think there's no room left for any more love, one can never underestimate the affection felt by everyone involved for Tolkien's original text and the determination to do his legacy the justice it truly deserves.

GARY RUSSELL
CARDIFF, 2007

The JOURNEY BEGINS

I t's Friday 22nd August, 2005, and on the car radio a man is discussing the US plane-crash series, *Lost*. He comments that the token Brit is a bit of a bad guy, prone to substance abuse and bouts of intense cowardice. "The usual American view of a Brit," the radio guy says. "Ah," says his co-host, "but he's not really a Brit, he's actually a hobbit!" They go on to talk about the actor as if he really is a hobbit. Not once is he named (it's Dominic Monaghan, of course, who played Merry in the movie trilogy). To the world at large, he's forever a hobbit.

Such is the price of fame, one supposes – take part in one of the most successful movie franchises ever, and that's what you'll always be remembered for: being a hobbit. One wonders if the same fate will befall Dylan Roberts, who has just been cast to play Merry in the first run of the stage production. Probably not – the mass audiences who gravitate towards movies and television are rarely replicated on the stage. And whilst a good few million people around the world have seen *The Phantom of the Opera*, *Mamma Mia* or *The Lion King*, ninety per cent of them would be hard pressed to remember anyone other than the headlining stars' names, and certainly not their faces. Of course, the theatre craft isn't about fame and fortune, but the events unfolding this day just outside the little eighteenth-century market town of Haverhill in Suffolk will, one suspects, result in something far more memorable than a hobbit.

Haverhill is a strange place: originally settled in Roman times, it was burned down during the seventeenth century and mostly rebuilt a hundred years later. As a result, it's a curious mishmash of styles, most of them pleasing but the odd eleventh-century bit of stonework

Previous The Black Rider (Nicholas Gede-Lange) enters during the original Toronto production.

Opposite Ready for the journey ahead: the four hobbits share a moment before starting their adventure. Frodo (James Loye, *seated*) is accompanied by (*left to right*) Merry (Richard Henders), Pippin (Owen Sharpe) and Sam (Peter Howe).

THE OFFICIAL STAGE COMPANION

often sits next to something a good deal younger. And sometimes older. It has a timeless nature as a result, a nature that the big modern industrial estates, carefully built in a ring around the town itself, can do nothing to despoil. It's strangely appropriate that somewhere so wonderfully indefinable is currently playing host to another timeless, ageless location: Middle-earth. This is where, once it has been transported to Toronto in Canada, the likes of the aforementioned Mr Roberts and his fellow thespians will be bringing to life the most ambitious, most daring and most breathtaking (and quite possibly also the most expensive-to-produce) theatrical spectacular of all time.

You see, Haverhill is the hometown of a company called Delstar and it has been their job to create and construct the amazing revolving, lifting circular stage upon which *The Lord of the Rings* will be played out over its three-hour running time. And, for the last couple of weeks, a small army of people from the production have based

All the good choreography work that Peter Darling, Rob Tannion, Alex Frith and their team have put in is shown to good effect during rehearsals, as the Orcs of the original Toronto cast leap around the constantly shifting stage.

themselves in one of Delstar's aircraft-hangar-sized buildings to go through, well, the motions.

The stage itself is a raised dais, fourteen metres in diameter and weighing thirty-five tons. It's terribly impressive, rotates in both directions and consists of seventeen lifts that can attain varying heights during the course of a performance. It will be the bridge of Khazad-dûm. It will be Helm's Deep. It will be Mount Doom. Indeed, about the only thing it won't be is flat and immobile, which is both good fun and rather daunting. Today is the last day everyone will have the chance to play with it before it gets dismantled piece by piece, carefully wrapped up and shipped over to Toronto, where it will then be carefully installed in the Princess of Wales theatre ready for rehearsals. A gang of Delstar's technicians and carpenters are on hand throughout the day's planning sessions, making the tiniest adjustments whenever necessary. Lift 16 is causing some concern today, as every time it rises to form part of the battlements for an Orc battle that Rob Tannion and Alex Frith are trying to choreograph it clunks alarmingly into the lift beside it. A bit of jiggery pokery involving a hammer, a saw and a couple of expletives and it's fixed.

"Let's go again," set and costume designer Rob Howell yells out. A young Canadian guy called Kevin Dixon is staring at an iBook, pressing keys as the sequence is input. He's very concerned at the clunking that's been going on. He sets the battlements off in motion again.

With the fourteen-metre stage installed at Delstar, it is time for Alex and his fellow "Orcs" to see what is possible, and safe, to achieve when you're equipped with two crutches.

THE OFFICIAL STAGE COMPANION

Orcs from the original Toronto cast gather in line, hunched menacingly over their weapon-crutches, ready to charge their foe.

Two minutes later and 'Clunk,' responds Lift 16 rather unhelpfully. Kevin sighs. It's proving to be one of those days.

But no one seems too worried. They know that the Delstar chaps will have it jiggered and pokered before director Matthew Warchus (the leader of this particular, if you like, fellowship) can polish off his plastic pot of salad. Sure enough, moments later, Lift 16 finally rises gracefully up, enabling Rob, Alex and their team of performers to leap around with Orc-like grace, practising their jumps from one lift to another with the aid of crutches that have been customised with wicked-looking blades upon the shafts. Nice guys these Orcs, clearly.

Next to Kevin is a whole bank of iBooks, a mission control for Middle-earth – production coordinator Jane Thompson keeps everything ticking over, while Rob Howell's team of associate designers, Megan Huish and Andrzej Goulding, are working out

EITHER WAY, THIS DAY AT DELSTAR IS BUZZING WITH ENERGY AND ENTHUSIASM – MOST OF THESE PEOPLE HAVE BEEN WORKING ON THE PROJECT FOR NEARLY TWO YEARS NOW, BUT THERE'S NO SIGN OF WEARINESS OR FRACTIOUSNESS.

specific lifts and rotates for other scenes. Next to them is sound designer Simon Baker, who is keeping a careful eye on where people will be standing to maximise the acoustic advantages of the theatre, and mentally balancing the sound of the lifts with speech and music. Everyone's fingers are flicking across keyboards, or scribbling down notes. Matthew Warchus at one point takes a video call over Megan's computer from someone on the other side of the Atlantic who has just got up. Or maybe they haven't been to bed yet. Either way, this day at Delstar is buzzing with energy and enthusiasm – most of these people have been working on the project for nearly two years now, but there's no sign of weariness or fractiousness. Just an unwavering enthusiasm for what is being achieved, the new ground being broken and the bar being raised another few notches in live theatre spectaculars.

An early idea for the prologue was a shadow-play recounting how Bilbo obtained the Ring from Gollum.

The DIRECTOR

or Matthew Warchus, it's been an unusual journey. Directors rarely give themselves over to projects on this scale, where their entire life is taken up by just one solitary production. But it's a sacrifice he feels is worth it.

"In the spring of 2002, I think," he says, as we discuss when he actually got his feet under the table of *The Lord of the Rings*. "I was living in New York when I had a visit from Kevin Wallace. He said he had a project I might be interested in and, in a secretive way, handed me the script of *The Lord of the Rings* and some music CDs – I didn't know the book, although I had once read *The Hobbit*, so I started reading the script on the subway home. A period of about four months passed during which I was very sceptical about the whole idea, uncertain about the particular approach the script was taking; and more so about the music he had given me. So you could say I didn't immediately respond positively. But Kevin gave me time to read the book, do some thinking, and a great deal more of talking to him. When I came back to London I told him that I could see a way of doing *The Lord of the Rings* on stage, but different in so many ways from the direction the script was going in. And yes, I said I was up for directing it... almost – I was still not a hundred per cent convinced. I was equivocating about the scale of it – I mean, I could see that this was going to be a project that completely dominated

Inset Director Matthew Warchus.

Opposite For the original Toronto production, the Fellowship arrive in the Elven domain of Lothlórien, climbing up into the safety of the mighty Mallorn trees in which the Elves live. This design would ultimately evolve for the London production.

THE OFFICIAL STAGE COMPANION

WE'RE NOT USED TO BEING COMPLETELY IMMERSED IN JUST ONE THING FOR THAT LENGTH OF TIME. IT WAS A BIG RESPONSIBILITY BECAUSE IT WOULD BE UNDER SUCH A LOT OF SCRUTINY – IT'S AN AUDACIOUS THING TO DO ON ITS OWN TERMS, LET ALONE IN COMPARISON WITH THE FILMS.

the life of whoever took it on. As a freelance director you're used to taking on lots of work, three or four projects in a given year: opera, film, plays, musicals. We're not used to being completely immersed in just one thing for that length of time. It was a big responsibility because it would be under such a lot of scrutiny – it's an audacious thing to do on its own terms, let alone in comparison with the films.

"So although there were many reasons for saying no, after reading the book I started to get a vision of how the theatre could take the material and run with it, doing all the things that theatre does best, using spectacle, using music. Theatre is a very emotional phenomenon – at its best it picks up the audience and moves them, transports them on flights of imagination, in an environmental way that cinema doesn't do; with movies, you're more passive, an observer. So I thought this could be overwhelming, and a huge burden of responsibility, but it could also result in the kind of theatre that I like. I've always been drawn to material that's visceral and emotional, strong archetypal dramas between characters, which it's got. I also like magic. I often try to use illusions in my productions – with *The Lord of the Rings* there's plenty of scope for that. Also, I trained in music, so I'm keen on the use of music and sound. Here was a project where fantasy and the supernatural would be coexisting with very real psychological concerns and relationships. All entwined. It's tricky, because I realised it could become exactly the kind of thing I became a director in order to do and yet it was going to be extremely taxing. But in the end, I couldn't find enough good reasons to say no!"

Opposite Aragorn and Gimli bear the brunt of an Orc attack (*top*) during the original Toronto production, while (*bottom*) all is peaceful as the wandering Elves greet their Hobbit fellow travellers.

The WRITER

An involvement stretching back to early 2002 actually makes Matthew a babe in arms compared to how long others have been involved in the gestation period of staging *The Lord of the Rings*. Unsurprisingly, producer Kevin Wallace goes back further than Matthew, but not even his involvement can equal that of co-writer Shaun McKenna, for whom it started with a tent in Berlin. Sort of...

"Like everybody else, I suppose, I read the book around the time it first came out in paperback at the end of the Sixties. My third-year English teacher said, 'Oh, if you want a really good read, I recommend *The Lord of the Rings*,' and I thought, 'Yeah, yeah, yeah... old fart. Nobody's going to read that.' It also looked very big, and anyway I was very snobby about fantasy as a teenager. So I didn't read it until after I'd just graduated. I was living in Bristol and somebody in my house was reading the thing. It was one of the first books I read after doing my English degree where I didn't check to see what page I was on and whether I was going to get it read by next week, so it was actually a labour of love. I think I read it twice – we were all very into it and just sat in the pub and had conversations about, when we made our definitive film of *The Lord of the Rings*, all our friends were going to be in it. I was always very disappointed because, of course, I naturally wanted to be Gandalf or Aragorn... and everyone said, 'Shaun, you can be Tom Bombadil.' I thought, 'No way! I want to be heroic.' Later on, I saw the Ralph Bakshi cartoon film when it came out but I was never, well, a fanatical Tolkien follower, which I think actually has proved to be beneficial to this project.

I WAS ALWAYS VERY DISAPPOINTED BECAUSE, OF COURSE, I NATURALLY WANTED TO BE GANDALF OR ARAGORN... AND EVERYONE SAID, 'SHAUN, YOU CAN BE TOM BOMBADIL.' I THOUGHT, 'NO WAY! I WANT TO BE HEROIC.'

"You see, I simply thought that it was a great book, one that could be recommended to kids. Then, years later, I went to a meeting – this must have been either 1998 or 1999 and, to be honest, I hadn't thought about *The Lord of the Rings* for ages. It was a lunch at The Ivy with a director called Stuart Wood, who I was working with on another show. In fact, I think we were just negotiating the fees to do this other show, and it came up over lunch that he was also doing *The Lord of the Rings*. I joked, 'Who's doing that? That's my job. I have to write that.' And he replied, 'Okay!' So, that was really how it came about. Then I met John Havu, who had the rights to stage a live performance of the book. Now, all this goes back to some years earlier, when musical producer Bernd Stromberger had done, in a tent in Berlin, a production of *The Lord of the Rings*, for which he'd somehow managed to get the rights. He'd

Opposite Writer Shaun McKenna.

Below One of the many challenges for the team was to be faithful to the book while also emotionally engaging the audience through both spoken word and song, as performed here by the original Toronto cast.

written all the music, written all the lyrics, designed the costumes and directed it. John Havu was one of the producers, and the urban myth is that it had been funded by Russian Mafia money. Whether that's true or not, it was a bit of a disaster and it all went terribly, terribly wrong. The sets and costumes weren't paid for, so they didn't turn up. Bernd is a talented composer, but he shouldn't have done everything else as well. Also, he hadn't actually done *The Lord of the Rings* anyway; he'd done *The Hobbit* and called it *The Lord of the Rings*. Stuart had gone out to see if he could save it, but eventually they all came to the conclusion that it wasn't a question of saving, it was a question of starting again. So I met John, I met Bernd, and we looked at what he'd got and what could be cannibalised out of it. He and Stuart had done a sort of treatment, a sort of outline, but this only featured five in the Fellowship!

"I thought they couldn't do that, and started work on a new script. Bernd wanted to do it sung-through but I'm allergic to sung-through musicals, I really don't understand why people have to sing 'Would you like a cup of tea?'. I just don't get it – and anyway it takes forever to do plot in sung-through. Also, I've never seen a sung-through musical where the characters were more than paper-thin.

"I remember one weekend I had to travel to Devon so I listened to the BBC radio dramatisation, which is 13 hours long, all the way down to Devon and all the way back. Then I reread the books, and was struck by how the characters were, in some ways, really pure archetypes – Frodo, for instance. He is an incredibly passive hero, which works well in the context of the book, because as you read it you become Frodo; you identify with him; you give Frodo your characteristics. But as a dramatic, functional leading character in another medium... well, it lacks something.

"John had the rights to do it in Switzerland and Germany, I think. He'd made contact with Laurie Battle at Tolkien Enterprises and she was putting her notes in, and we did lots and

Opposite Many variations of facial prosthetic were tried out for Frodo's appearance, in order to perfect the look. Here, James Loye has had his eyebrows blocked out and false ones painted in.

Below When Frodo puts on the Ring for the first time he is plunged into a nightmare twilight world where he is suddenly visible to the searching gaze of the Dark Lord, Sauron.

THE OFFICIAL STAGE COMPANION

I WAS DETERMINED TO BE RESISTANT TO THE WHOLE MYTHOLOGY SUCKING ME IN – IF YOU STEP OFF THE EDGE OF THE CLIFF, YOU COULD BE IN THERE FOR THE REST OF YOUR LIFE.

lots of work on it. Of course, this was all before we even knew there was definitely going to be a movie version. We knew it was being talked about, but we certainly didn't know there were going to be three, or just how big a phenomenon it was going to be.

"Anyway, gradually, we gave up on the production being sung-through but we were still very much writing in the conventions of a musical, because that was the brief. And Bernd wrote some songs. Bernd's style is quite heavily influenced by Euro-pop, and it became clear that he actually couldn't write big theatrical stuff, so we got in Stephen Keeling, who I've worked with a lot, and still work with – my composer of choice – to write the music. Over the course of a couple of years, we created very much a musical-theatre version, with some lovely songs in it.

A close-up view of Bilbo Baggins' front door at Bag End, pictured against the Toronto auditorium; stepping outside puts Frodo on the path to adventure.

"John then approached Kevin Wallace, because John is not a rich man and he was trying to raise the money to pay us; Kevin was experienced at producing on a large-scale and he had introduced Stuart to Bernd in the first place. Had this been anything else I'd have said, 'Thank you and goodnight.' But I didn't want to lose *The Lord of the Rings*; we'd all got terribly attached to it and invested a great deal of ourselves in it. It's such an amazing work – it's taken a long time and a lot of re-readings to understand its depth and complexity, because although I think the characters are paper-thin, they're in fact quite subtly drawn. Because of the way he wrote, and the things he drew upon, there's a whole universe to explore, but I was very wary of stepping into that any more than I needed to. I was determined to be resistant to the whole mythology sucking me in – if you step off the edge of the cliff, you could be in there for the rest of your life. Despite all that, I had indeed become very attached to it and so Kevin, Stephen and I started to find ways of putting a lot of things back into the story that had not been in Bernd's original treatment. With every pass, we came closer to Tolkien's original work. This is all before it got into its current form, when Matthew was brought on board…"

THE OFFICIAL STAGE COMPANION

The PRODUCER

The selection of the director of this particular Fellowship leads us neatly to the producer of this stage production, Kevin Wallace. He joined the project as Shaun explained, some time after the writer, but his pedigree goes back quite some way, firstly as an accomplished theatre actor, and then moving behind the scenes with Andrew Lloyd-Webber's internationally renowned Really Useful Group of theatre producers. Kevin's a rarity in British mainstream, or West End, theatre. He's an independent. Kevin Wallace Productions is emerging, however, as a production company to rival not just Really Useful, but also Bill Kenwright, The Ambassador Group, Cameron Mackintosh and all the other major players in the heart of London's theatreland. A charming Irishman in his early forties, Kevin moved into theatre production after some years as a successful actor and *The Lord of the Rings* seems set to be his biggest success yet. But as Kevin explains, getting to the state of actually having actors performing on the stage has been a long, laborious and frequently tricky journey...

"I worked with RUG from 1994 until 2001. My first job for them was to go out to Germany and Switzerland to set up two separate subsidiaries – one to do *The Phantom of the Opera* in Switzerland, and one to do *Sunset Boulevard* in Germany. It was an amazing job to do because there was absolutely nothing set up, nothing there at all. RUG had started to build these theatres; they'd done the deals to stage these productions by licensing them to co-producers in those territories, and had hired me to go out and set up the ticketing, the marketing and the whole commercial side of it.

So of course I brought on board a load of people to help me do all that, and one of them was John Havu, who at that time was playing in the band on the Zürich production of *Cats*. He wanted to move into the management side of orchestral management, and his pitch to me was that, because he knew the musicians in Germany and Switzerland, he would book them. I was happy to let him deal with that side of things.

"So, after that, I came back to London and was appointed Head of the Really Useful Group's theatre production division. This meant I was responsible for all the copyrights around the world, which is a wonderful job. It also meant that I was closely involved in the creative process with Lloyd-Webber, because when he was doing a new show I was the in-house producer given the task of bringing those shows to the stage.

"Anyway, I had kept in touch with John and he told me that he had met Bernd Stromberger, who had this limited licence from Laurie Battle and from Tolkien Enterprises to do what was essentially a

Above Members of the ensemble cast perform as Rangers: in this sequence, the combination of thoroughly rehearsed choreography by Peter Darling, Rob Howell's strong visual design, evocative costumes and the striking lighting design by Paul Pyant work together to transport the audience to Middle-earth. Teamwork is the essential ingredient that has enabled the production to succeed.

Opposite The producer, Kevin Wallace.

THE OFFICIAL STAGE COMPANION

production of *The Hobbit*, in German, and he was doing it in a tent in a field in Berlin. Now, Bernd actually called it *Der Herr der Ringe – The Lord of the Rings* – but they got in trouble with their audiences because, as Shaun mentioned, what they were really doing was a version of *The Hobbit*.

"John initially became involved by offering to supply the band for them, but as time went by he got more heavily involved in the staging, in a sort of associate-producer capacity, because the production was having problems. And because John and I kept in touch, he told me all about them: Stromberger had decided he was going to direct this piece himself, which clearly meant he'd taken too much on. He'd written the music, he'd done the adaptation, so he was already heavily involved in the production – as well as too much. So John said to me that they needed to find somebody who could sort out the direction.

"As an actor, back in the late Eighties, I'd worked with a guy called Stuart Wood and Stuart was now doing stuff around London as a director, on the fringe, and a lot of work in drama schools. Because he had always had an interest in musicals, I said to John that I thought Stuart would be a good choice. He was somebody who would be prepared to go out to Germany and have a go at sorting this out for them; who wouldn't say, 'I'm not taking on someone else's work,' and all that big ego stuff. So I introduced Stuart to John, and sure enough Stuart got heavily involved in it, and then they wanted to rewrite it, so Stuart introduced Shaun McKenna to John and they all went off to Berlin and they tried to save Bernd Stromberger's Hobbit-in-a-tent. Unfortunately, it sank without trace – it just didn't work. But they'd all got to know one another – so while they were out there, this combination of Havu and Stromberger and McKenna and Wood thought, 'Wouldn't it be nice to do it properly?'

"What they should have done was a pure adaptation of *The Lord of the Rings*. So, John

Opposite Gollum (Michael Therriault) attacks Sam (Peter Howe) but is in turn threatened by the sword Sting, wielded by Frodo.

Below The Toronto Barliman Butterbur (Shawn Wright), innkeeper of *The Prancing Pony*, peers out to see who is knocking on his door at such a late hour.

THE OFFICIAL STAGE COMPANION

started talking to Laurie about a licence for *The Lord of the Rings* – at this point he was talking about a version for Switzerland, which is where he was based, and the possibility of a tour of the UK. Now, this was at a point way before the films had come onto the cinema screens; we're back in early 2000. John was talking to Laurie about a level of licence that Laurie would have done before, when they licensed Vanessa Ford to do *The Hobbit* in the UK. They had also licensed another lady to do a large puppet-version in Australia. It was that modest level of licence they were looking at.

"Then, in August 2001, I left The Really Useful Group and set up myself as an independent producer. Beforehand I had told John that any of my creative copyrights were under contract to Really Useful, and therefore I couldn't get involved at all in his adventure with Bernd and the tent. But when I left Really Useful John told me about the situation that he was in now. He'd managed to keep the whole thing alive and ticking over with Laurie and he was continuing to talk about this Swiss licence, and he then gave me a copy of Shaun McKenna's draft script.

"At the time I was reading lots of scripts; as an independent producer scripts were being thrust under my nose on a daily basis.

Frodo faces a difficult decision, whether to go on alone on his quest to destroy the Ring, and break the Fellowship. Here, the four hobbits of the original Toronto production are all wearing their magical cloaks given to them by Galadriel at Lothlórien.

When I read this, it was a script that I found myself turning the pages of, and being emotionally engaged with the characters, and engaged in the situation and lost in the world that was on the page. Of course, this sounds like the absolute minimum requirement for any script, but the fact is that most of the scripts you read don't actually achieve anything like that. But this did. I was intrigued, because Shaun had found a way of taking the thousand pages of Tolkien and getting to the heart of the story, putting it onto the page in his very first draft. It was there; he'd found a way of doing that.

BUT WHEN I READ THIS, IT WAS A SCRIPT THAT I FOUND MYSELF TURNING THE PAGES OF, AND BEING EMOTIONALLY ENGAGED WITH THE CHARACTERS, AND ENGAGED IN THE SITUATION AND LOST IN THE WORLD THAT WAS ON THE PAGE.

"John asked me, 'Are you interested in getting involved?' and I said I was, but he then showed me this draft agreement licence that he had from Tolkien Enterprises. Because of the experience I'd had at Really Useful regarding global licensing, of brand creation within the context of commercial theatre, and the development of new copyrights, I was sensitive to the value of the creation of copyright and knew what you needed to do in terms of securing them. He showed me the licence and it was basically the sort of licence that Tolkien Enterprises would have given to a school: 'You do the show; if you adapt it we own the material; give it back to us when you've finished; you don't own anything, and you've no rights beyond the performances you're going to do.'

"I explained to John that if I was going to get involved I wanted to create copyright – this was why I'd gone out by myself, why I'd become an independent. I was interested in a version of *The Lord of the Rings* that would be an international copyright in a first-class context. A version where one would go out and find the most appropriate creative team available in the genre of theatre, and create a production that would play in all the principal markets. A version that, ten years down the road, when people were listing the elite

Overleaf The original Toronto cast perform as marauding Orcs at Helm's Deep.

Opposite Elrond (Victor A. Young) descends to calm the raging waters during the dramatic scene at the Ford of Bruinen.

productions they would say: *'The Phantom of the Opera, The Lion King, The Lord of the Rings'* – a version synonymous with that level of quality and that scale of production, that profile, and hopefully that level of artistic and commercial success.

"So I did a deal with John to acquire the rights to Shaun McKenna's draft, and then he introduced me to Laurie, and we had a conversation, and she said to me she wasn't the person to talk to any more. She passed me on to Al Bendich and ultimately to Norman Rudman. Norman is the lawyer for Saul Zaentz, and he had apparently negotiated the film deal between Saul and New Line Cinema. Norman dealt with the type of licences that I was envisaging. Norman could see that the licence John Havu had was wholly inappropriate for the scale of show I was talking about so we just started over again. He asked me what I wanted…

"When I was at RUG I always enjoyed the dual aspects of production: of both creative producing and the business side of it. I had sat in on all the negotiations for *Phantom* for Mexico, for Copenhagen, etcetera, and sat there with Jonathan Hull, the in-house RUG lawyer, and with the business boys, and we all worked very closely together. Based on all that experience I'd acquired, I sat down and wrote a

Below One of Saruman's Orcs (Tyler Murree), preparing to go out into battle against the people of Rohan under the banner of the White Wizard.

business proposal for Norman, creating *The Lord of the Rings* as a piece of commercial, musical theatre, and then replicating it around the world. I was asking for an exclusive licence.

"I was well aware that these productions cost in the region of six to eight million pounds, but if that's the kind of money one's going to be raising, staging that level of production, you can't have a production opening in London if someone else has the rights to open a different one in New York. I wanted the rights to open it in London and, if it's successful in London, take it around the world.

"I sent that proposal to Norman in early 2002, got a positive response and then a

meeting was set up with Saul Zaentz. But not until May! Saul was that busy. Then there was a slight hiccup regarding the dates – they couldn't actually give me the licence until early 2003, after the second movie had hit the theatres; I presume that this related in some way to their agreement with New Line Cinema. Whatever it meant, it gave me a year to get things moving, so that when I went back to Saul it would be with a proposal that really showed him we knew what we were doing, that we meant business. It would prove that we were the right people to grant the licence to.

"It's very easy to announce to people, 'We're going to do this and it'll be terrific and spectacular,' but it's hard to back that up if they've not read Shaun's script. I also needed to move quickly because I was aware that if I thought it was a good idea, especially with the success of the movie, someone else might think that too. And after all the work that had gone into it I was determined not to lose out to someone else. That meant demonstrating that what we offered was the absolute best thing possible. I had a year to sort that out.

Members of the creative team pose for the cameras during floor testing at Delstar. Two of the team are wearing the sprung stilts that will allow the performers to lope and leap across the stage.

Left In full Orc costume, the performers (Troy Feldman and Joe Eigo) rear up on their stilts for maximum menace.

"This was making me nervous because there are some very big players in the business, whereas I'm an independent. However, I think this probably worked to my advantage in that Saul is a fiercely independent producer and he responded favourably to the fact that I'm fiercely independent too – we don't work within the corporate structure. But I still thought, 'We've got to really consolidate this, get this script up to scratch.'

"So we continued working on the script, and Bernd Stromberger had written some music along with Stephen Keeling, so we produced a demo CD. This was a significant financial investment for a fledgling independent company, but I believed that, if you had the opportunity to secure the stage rights to *The Lord of the Rings*, a once-in-a-lifetime opportunity, you couldn't walk away from it; you had to keep pouring money into it. So we continued to work on the script, we did this CD and I continued to have conversations with Laurie Battle. Laurie was heavily involved in the continuing evolution of the adaptation and was giving us very sound advice in terms of the shaping of the script, because her knowledge, her deep understanding of Tolkien's work, is invaluable.

Below A sculpture of an Orc head produced during the conceptual design process, with painted helmet and fitted mouth-brace.

THE OFFICIAL STAGE COMPANION

"At the beginning of February 2003, I flew out to Berkeley and we met up and everything seemed to go well. First off, I met up with Laurie, who was surrounded by every piece of merchandise that's ever been created for the films, so her office looked more like a toyshop! I'd got to know Laurie quite well during all our phone calls and exchanges and she knew how important the whole thing was to me; she'd been an amazing supporter of the project, indeed of me, and we've become great friends. Then I headed up to Saul's office, and Al came in and we had the actual conversation. Now, with these sorts of pitches, you know that this is the most important thing in the world to you, but you're also mindful of the fact that for the people who are in the room with you, this is just one more thing in their business day and they probably have ten other things to deal with. So, you're monitoring as you're talking, checking that everyone's remaining focused, interested, that there's a potential compatibility, that you are all on the same wavelength – all those things are running through your mind as you're making your pitch. You're just hoping it's not all going to come crashing down around your ears!"

Frodo and Sam encounter the Rangers who, under the captaincy of Aragorn, have been secretly protecting the hobbits from Sauron's forces.

NOT LONG AFTER, WE BEGAN A DELIGHTFUL PERIOD
OF TRADING EMAILS BACK AND FORTH, EXPLORING
THE CHARACTERS AND THEIR RELATIONSHIPS,
CREATING A BODY OF MATERIAL FOR SHAUN TO
WORK FROM IN REFINING THE SCRIPT.

So, how did it look from the other side? Laurie Battle, whom
Kevin mentioned, has been the Creative Consultant from Tolkien
Enterprises for a long time now. This means she's effectively the
guardian of the commercial end of Tolkien's work, ensuring that
everything from action figures to plates, from limited edition bronze
sculptures of Ents through to highly detailed paintings of
Weathertop all go past her for approval. And before that approval is
given there may come a lengthy but invaluable period of suggestions
for tweaking this, amending that, ensuring that Tolkien's work and
reputation are never cheapened, never sullied. It's a job that requires
not just an encyclopedic knowledge of every word Tolkien wrote, but
a love of Middle-earth and, at the same time, one of the most
extraordinarily canny commercial minds in the business. Laurie
knows what will and won't work regarding exploiting *The Lord of the
Rings*, and clearly, like so many others, she saw something in Shaun
McKenna's early scripts.

"Two things stand out in my memories of that early draft script.
One is how well Shaun had structured the story – I immediately
appreciated that it is no mean feat to distill the infinitely complex
narrative of *The Lord of the Rings* down into a cohesive, compelling
evening's entertainment. Shaun's cheerful response to criticism was
also impressive. My initial reactions were about two-thirds 'Here's
why this isn't consistent with what Tolkien wrote' and one-third
'Here's why this doesn't work from a contemporary Californian/
female perspective'. As I was so busy on other fronts, I'm afraid my
written comments were rather rushed and blunt. In response, John,
Stuart and Shaun set up a phone conference, and we brainstormed
at length about the script and the project's potential. Shaun pro-
claimed that collaboration was what he loved about doing musical
theatre, and welcomed my further input.

"Not long after, we began a delightful period of trading emails back and forth, exploring the characters and their relationships, creating a body of material for Shaun to work from in refining the script. Kevin's arrival on the scene brought a heightened degree of professionalism, but he graciously nurtured what I viewed as a 'Hey kids, let's put on a show!' tone in Shaun's and my exchanges.

"When Matthew joined up in early 2003, I realized that while he would introduce new flavours into the mix, his approach to the story matched my instinct for how it needed to be told. Treating *The Lord of the Rings* as an epic that chronicles ancient legends would honour Tolkien's premise that the *Red Book of Westmarch* was a historical manuscript. A manuscript that had survived down through the ages and landed in his hands, while providing the artistic freedom to tell the story in a new way. The key would be in bringing the characters to life by having their actions, motivations and relationships be consistent with what was already known about them. If the script could remain true to that, we would be able to show them in settings that didn't appear in the books, and even to portray different ways that certain events might have taken place. The primary focus would be on telling a good story rather than on trying to figure out how we could cram all of *The Lord of the Rings* into an evening's entertainment.

"An alchemy soon emerged in the crafting of the script. Shaun would send the latest draft, I would read it through and note my initial reactions, and then work through it more slowly documenting my comments with excerpts from the text of *The Lord of the Rings*, as well as Tolkien's letters, or his extended writings. I also surveyed the vast body of scholarly writings on Tolkien and Middle-earth and quoted passages that rang true for the points I wanted to make. Shaun and Matthew would then respond to my feedback and indeed several trips over to London helped to cement a fast-paced, fun working relationship. It's worth noting that without the miracles of modern technology - email, faxes, air travel, etc. - to assist the flow of communication, we would never have been able to draw from such a deep well of source material."

As Laurie mentioned the script, that brings us neatly back to another of our very own Fellowship, writer Shaun McKenna, who has his own definite ideas about what makes the story tick.

The SCRIPT

"The heart of the book for me was what I remembered and loved, and still love, from that very first read back in Bristol. It's the whole Frodo, Sam and Gollum triangle. I think Gollum is just the most amazing creation, a wonderful character. He's the definitive addict. My wife was an addiction counsellor, and in a lot of the other scripts I've written I've looked at the nature of addiction a lot. So that was a hook I knew about and could recognise. It's his whole desperately wanting something, and his complete inability to control his need for it, even though it's the worst thing he could possibly have, and the lengths that it will drive him to. So that was always, for me, the emotional heart of the story and that was the part that was at the centre of the version that I was going to tell.

"The next layer down was Gandalf and Aragorn, and then it was a question of working down through everyone else's stories – in everything I've done, it's always been important to me that every character gets a journey, however small. If they've only got one scene, they need a journey in that scene. That may explain why, in those early drafts, we didn't have the Ents, because we didn't see how we could do them well, and give them that journey. Similarly, we didn't include in the first version anything of Théoden or Helm's Deep or the Riders of Rohan. Once the Fellowship split, we kept up with Aragorn now and again, just to keep his part of the plot going, but all that military conflict in Rohan had to go. Plus, of course, in *The Lord of the Rings* there are a number of battles and you can only really have one.

"Before we got too far into adapting the text, John took it to Kevin, who, after 'umming' and 'ahhing' for a time, said he thought it could possibly be done. So Bernd and Stephen Keeling and Stuart

Opposite During the original Toronto production Gandalf (Brent Carver) counsels the hobbits, Merry and Pippin, not to believe everything that they hear: the tongues of Sauron's henchmen are coated with lies. This scene would ultimately be cut for the London production.

THE OFFICIAL STAGE COMPANION

and I continued working for probably the best part of another year – while Kevin went off to convince Saul Zaentz. Laurie Battle had always liked the scripts and been supportive, and given her input and guided us when we made changes she thought were contrary to the spirit of the book. I guess we spent another nine months doing version after version, and by now of course this was Kevin's complete musical-theatre version, which he took to Saul and said, 'This is what we want to do and would he give us the rights?' It took a while, but Saul eventually said yes… depending on who's directing it. You see, there needed to be something else to convince him of the quality of the people Kevin could attract to be involved in the project: I wasn't a star writer; none of the composers were star composers; it meant it really had to be the director. There was much discussion of who would be the right person to do it, and eventually Kevin talked to Matthew Warchus and Matthew agreed to do it and came on board – and then it all changed again.

KEVIN WALLACE *ON* MATTHEW WARCHUS

I believe that Matthew was the most appropriate director in the English-speaking world to direct *The Lord of the Rings*. He has extraordinary intellectual rigour and a love for the power of the theatre – an almost child-like belief in the power and wonder of theatre, and of the capacity of play to engage an audience with actors – combined with his experience of being able to do large-scale productions, both musicals and plays, and his renowned use of classical text in a contemporary environment. His Shakespeares are so successful because, when you go and watch a Warchus production of a Shakespeare, those characters still speak beautifully in Shakespeare's language but sound like they're actually speaking real words to each other; and that has an immediacy to it. So for all those reasons, and because he's of a generation which is still fresh and hungry, I believed if I could hook him into *The Lord of the Rings* he would give the amount of time that this would need. Other directors of the generation beyond him will say they have too much on their plates and wouldn't give you what has turned out to be nearly three years of preparation and creative commitment.

ACTUALLY, THE VERSION THAT WE HAD WORKED
VERY NICELY AS A PIECE OF PURE MUSICAL THEATRE,
BUT MATTHEW FELT QUITE STRONGLY THAT IT
SHOULDN'T OBEY ANY OF THE CONVENTIONS OF
ANY GENRE.

"Matthew thought long and hard about how we were all very aware that the idea of 'The Lord of the Rings: The Musical' was naff. Actually, the version that we had worked very nicely as a piece of pure musical theatre, but Matthew felt quite strongly that it should-n't obey any of the conventions of any genre. What we had at this stage, however, was very much in the musical-theatre genre, so there was some discussion about the style of the music. They did some workshops, trying to 'ethnicise' the existing music, which didn't really work, so it was decided to look for other composers – which was a huge shock. It made me very uneasy, as I didn't know whether I'd be the next to go, and in fact Keeling and I were out in Switzerland, where we were preparing a production of *Heidi*, when this call comes through to his mobile from Kevin effectively telling Keeling he's been sacked. Stephen and I were very depressed for the rest of the afternoon and I was angry, not knowing whether I was on the project or not, but as it turned out they thought that I was still the best choice of writer for the project.

"So Matthew and I started again, really, with this notion that the songs wouldn't do what songs do in musical theatre; instead they would be the old songs of Middle-earth; that people would sing them because they were singing the old songs. We would also try to include much more of the story of the book than we were doing, so this adaptation would be much less of a filleted version, and more complete – however, some scenes are pretty much as they were in the 1999 draft, just not always in the same place. We also played around with doing the show as a three-act version, then down to two acts, then back again. Even today I can't remember at which point we settled on a final script – draft 31, 32, something like that, although it was probably nearer 40!"

Matthew agrees with this, commenting that the amount of rewriting was exhausting but frequently necessary. The word 'organic' springs to mind – many of this 'Fellowship' use it not just to describe the visual and emotional aspects of the finished production, but the very journey of getting there. Things changed frequently, but never pointlessly. It's not unusual for the director of a project this size to take an interest in the script, or indeed the design, sound, music and everything else. But the level of hands-on involvement that Matthew experienced took him almost by surprise.

"When I read the book, and after reading the 'German' script, I went into the production with an open mind, wondering whether, perhaps, it should be a straight play or whether it should be done over three evenings; things like that. Eventually, I decided to assume it could be anything we want, and take it from there. When reading the book, the thing that surprised me most was that every so often someone actually breaks into song, be it Hobbits or Elves or Men or Dwarves. They're always singing songs, and Tolkien actually also describes the background music; in fact, he created a very musical world.

The simple rustic townfolk of Bree perform a lively dance routine at *The Prancing Pony* inn during the original Toronto production.

THE LORD OF THE RINGS

"So I thought that to tell the story without the music would be to cut something out of the material. Then there was the question of what kind of music; the answer seemed to be that it should come out of Tolkien's world rather than us making it an imposition. That's when I started to think that, instead of trying to pull Tolkien towards conventional musical theatre, the real trick was to pull conventional musical theatre towards Tolkien. We should make the sound of his voice present not only in the script but also in the music.

"His world is very textured, very organic, very folk-based and antiquated. So we decided to try to find music that wasn't reminiscent of something as secular or contemporary as *Les Miserables* or *The Phantom of the Opera* but would sound as, though recognisable, it might also come from a different world. Unusual and unique-sounding to our ears but satisfying at the same time. We drifted towards world music, and ultimately found music in India and Finland and combined the two.

"No matter how successful or how much I liked them, I knew I had to avoid doing *The Lord of the Rings* like the big mainstream shows. It would be a mismatch of that music and conventional music. I was thinking about productions of The Mystery Plays cycle I'd seen and the way the audience get involved in that sort of production.

THE OFFICIAL STAGE COMPANION

Also, the works of Peter Brook, like *Mahabharata*, Indian epics using a small group of actors in a small theatre, were shows with very simple, traditional storytelling devices. I also thought about *Nicholas Nickleby* – a group of actors using Poor Theatre style, where you're asking the audience to use their imagination to complete the picture. By getting the audience to build the world, you actually give them a bigger experience;

Above Director Matthew Warchus wanted everything about the design to be organically connected, "one living, breathing entity". Here a technician adds leaves and flowers to a metal-framed branch.

they feel more involved. On the other hand, I was thinking about *The Lion King*, and how it incorporated a very ethnic style musically and visually yet brings it all into the mainstream.

"So while it's not at all unusual for the director to be involved in all these areas, it was this early on in the process. In fact, normally the closest collaborative area is between the director and designer. But with my work in the past, I have always had more involvement

Right With the branch now secured with the others to the frame, it will now form part of the huge tree that descends and opens like a flower to act as a leafy canopy for the Fellowship at Lothlórien. Here it is tested under the watchful eyes of the production crew.

THE LORD OF THE RINGS

in the music than other directors might and I think that's because of my background – I'm just very interested in it. It's the same with scripts – I've had varying levels of input in creating a new piece, because you can get very involved in shaping the script; being live theatre, you're developing a whole production. But it is true to say that whatever I've done in the past, in this particular case my involvement has been much more extreme.

"I knew that, for a project of this scale, I'd be taking all this onboard. We're trying to make it a very holistic piece – the music needs to be entwined with the dialogue, all woven into each other, therefore the spoken parts of the script plus the lyrics and the instrumentations had to be worked through in parallel. They can't deviate and isolate that process, or amputate one from the other.

"Similarly with the design, I wanted everything organically connected, each aspect borne out of something else. I wanted the stage itself to be one living, breathing entity, all drawn from one thing, one

Frodo (James Loye) is menaced by the towering and terrifying figure of the chief of the Black Riders (Nicholas Gede-Lange) who are pursuing him in order to regain the Ring for their master, Sauron.

living event. Often shows suffer from a lack of integration – the design might not be quite right for a piece or the music was great but the script was weak and so on. Everybody knows that's unsatisfactory. So in trying to create the ideal, because in our case we've had the time to strive for that, then integration has been the ongoing goal all the way through. I think that there's an umbrella principle about this project so that everything new that comes in has to pass a test of 'how does it integrate?'. Will it stand out in the wrong way? Is it part of this world? So now everything we do – movement, choreography, magic, illusions, design, script, even casting – is now appraised as to whether it's 'of the world'. Ultimately, that's our response to Tolkien's world. I think the rigour that's gone into that is perhaps unusual but I think we've striven to do it because of real respect for the source material."

The WORKSHOPS

Part of that rigour has been the workshopping that has gone into the project. Workshops can be different things to different productions, but for *The Lord of the Rings* the whole gamut was run. There were workshops involving actors; workshops involving circus-skills performers; workshops for music; and workshops for dance and fight sequences. Kevin Wallace talks us through and the first of those workshops and why the process is so important.

"In September 2003, we gathered ten actors together – actors who we believed would, of course, do a good reading, but also would have opinions about what they were reading. These were people who I'd worked with before but more particularly people who Matthew had worked with before who he could trust. For two weeks, they read through the draft, the original draft, and of course this had been written in one particular way, which wasn't to Matthew's brief. But Shaun McKenna's extraordinarily fast, and like a chameleon in terms of how he writes.

One of the hobbit performers studies his new look: prosthetics were used to change the look of the nose, which in turn alters the whole face.

"I'll never forget the Monday when the actors gave their feedback on the script – they said it was tough going, and were laying into and challenging the text, and there were lots and lots of notes being generated both by them and Matthew. So, on the second night, McKenna absorbed all these notes then sat down and rewrote the first act. And it was read on the Wednesday morning. And this is what's remarkable about him as a writer: following their feedback, he turned himself into somebody else.

"Shaun does a lot of adaptations, so he had the capacity to absorb what Matthew was after in the change of tone, yet retain the principles of the story. So when it was read on the Wednesday by the actors, it now had the right tone that Warchus was after. It's gone through numerous adaptations since then but the key change was at that time, and McKenna absolutely earned his stripes on this project on that particular long night. We continued with that process in workshops that Matthew and the actors did, and at the end of two weeks we had a good draft of all three acts."

Matthew seems to have enjoyed the whole workshopping process enormously.

Alex Frith tests the first prototype of the Black Rider.

"We did three workshops, with three different casts over two years. If you don't do that, you run the risk of discovering something really nasty when you start to rehearse with the final cast. There'll be something that seemingly has one emotional shape on the page but once actors are involved you'll find that key moments will pull it in another direction entirely, so the workshops are crucial to avoid having that happen. It's unusual that we've had three opportunities to do that, but not unheard of. The workshops weren't full productions, though, because my job was to watch the whole, to see how everything worked rather than focusing on the performances. In those terms, you're only really skimming the surface of what the actors are doing. My focus at that time was to listen to the words, assess the music, be slightly detached and hear it in the abstract rather than focus on what the actors are bringing to it. I had to treat it almost like a radio performance so as to avoid the distractions. That said, we did see personalities emerging in the roles that we wanted to try to capture later. Also, performances by some of the people did strike me, and I was pleased, eighteen months later, to see them actually taking on the role.

"We joke about the Americans, saying that they workshop things to death, but they love it. As a result, things are often in development for years in America, whereas in the UK it is the norm for a show to get only minimal workshop time, which can be for different reasons.

THE OFFICIAL STAGE COMPANION

Laura Michelle Kelly rehearses for her role of Galadriel in the London production, when her character makes a spectacular entrance fit for an Elven queen.

Sometimes in a workshop the numbers will be sung very simply with a basic musical accompaniment in the room, to persuade people to invest in the show. Other times, it will be a proper workshop to do work on the text before you go into production.

"The scale of research and development on this, however, has been exceptional," adds Kevin. "I took a leaf out of Disney's approach to *The Lion King* as it was clear that they had gone through a relatively exhaustive process, as far as the physical production was concerned, before they started on stage. I believed that for *The Lord of the Rings*, because of the scale of what we were doing and because we were creating a unique physical world, it was going to be important to R and D some of those key elements in order to figure out how we were going to do them.

"What I want to leave after us, long after this particular production of *The Lord of the Rings* is memory is, in words and in music, a great adaptation of Tolkien's work, which can be taken by other creative teams, whether professionally or amateur in schools and colleges, and have new life breathed into it by them. Also, the principle of the words and the music are there for them to be able to release their imaginations, their creativity, their interpretation, and bring that interpretation to life for the audiences, because that was what I ultimately set out to do."

The adaptation is, of course, the basis for everything in the show. Matthew and Shaun are credited as co-writers for the production,

SOMETIMES IN A WORKSHOP THE NUMBERS WILL BE SUNG VERY SIMPLY WITH A BASIC MUSICAL ACCOMPANIMENT IN THE ROOM, TO PERSUADE PEOPLE TO INVEST IN THE SHOW.

even though Shaun's work precedes Matthew's involvement by quite a few years. Was this something that automatically happens with large-scale theatre productions? Shaun explains how they collaborated on the writing process:

"Matthew's input has been big enough to more than justify his credit. We actually sat down in the same room and worked on lyrics together, and in terms of the dialogue we would go through it word for word and comma for comma; he's incredibly detailed in the way he works. He's also very good at cutting, which is extremely useful, or saying, 'Why don't we just turn the whole thing upside-down and turn it inside-out and play around with it?' Whilst it's true I have done the majority of the writing, the result is very much the product of both Matthew and me, because of his vision of the production and the dramatic shape of the performance. His sense of this is very sound."

Laura tries on one of specially constructed lifts, which are worn by all the Elven characters to give them a suitably lofty appearance on the stage.

"Shaun was there from the start," says Matthew, "and it was his script I first read. I got into a dialogue with him, not realising how involved in the script I'd end up being, and as the dialogue went on, month by month, my involvement increased and our relationship became more than just a director talking to a writer. He was very understanding of that process."

"I remember being frowned at once," Shaun recalls; "and it concerned the Balrog. Writing the script you just say, 'A Balrog appears,' or later on, when Shelob arrives, it's 'a huge and ancient spider'. You think, 'Well, that's not my problem.' But it became so as the collaboration started and I began to consider

THE OFFICIAL STAGE COMPANION

Under the watchful eye of Alex Frith, one of the team performs a power-skip somersault sequence that will eventually makes its way into the show when the Orcs swarm across the stage.

those three words: 'A Balrog appears' actually translates in to quite a few minutes of stage time in something like this because it's an event, rather than just a character.

"Once we started working – and I love Matthew dearly now – it took quite a long time to bond because I was uncomfortable after what had happened with Keeling. And he's quiet. You have to wait for him, you can't rush him on anything; you can't say, 'Do you think this will be a good idea?' or, 'Bing-bang-bong, let's do this.' Instead, he will take you down a path, saying, 'What if we try this?' and you might spend two or three months exploring 'this' and then he'd say, 'No, we won't do that, we'll do something else.' Rob Howell had warned me about this – 'Just wait,' he said. 'Just go with him, and wait, and it will all come out right.' And that's exactly what happened: you go down a path and experiment with something and eventually either it merges organically into what's already working, or it doesn't and you abandon it and think, 'We can try this instead.' I learned to admire and respect him because he cared about that process.

"We had a few problems, not with each other, but with the process of adapting. The story has certain inherent structural dramatic problems, but we would find solutions to them. Then I'd go and see the next film as soon as it came out and realise they'd found the same solution, so therefore we couldn't use it, which was really annoying. One of the things we wanted to do was make Arwen more than just this rather vague figure that she is in the book, always seen at a distance. Obviously, Peter Jackson thought that as well, and he got over it by making her a kind of warrior princess – which meant we had to try to find all sorts of other ways to make her more interesting – but in my opinion they veered dangerously close to making her almost a sexist stereotype, so our Arwen ended up being cut back and cut back.

"I wouldn't say she's a weak character now, but she's a terribly difficult one to translate onto the stage, whereas in the book her ethereal role suits the printed page rather well. Another thing we learned is that, all the way down, there are lots of little doors in Tolkien's narrative, and if you open that door there's a whole path to go down. If you don't want to go down there, don't mention it at all – just leave it out. I recall that Peter Jackson said that just because some of the story isn't in the films it could still have happened, he just didn't show us that it was going on. We've taken that to heart as well, I think. Cutting certain bits out was quite easy; although I appreciate they'll always be someone's favourite bit of the story. We don't have Faramir, although his story is quite interesting, but all the Denethor stuff I just thought had no dramatic resonance. You see, this is actually one of the advantages of not being a complete Tolkien aficionado, because I could cut material without having any emotional attachment to it. I could just say that it doesn't work in the context of our production and so we're not glued to it. It's the same with the battle scenes – there were a number of them, spread throughout the book, but we condensed them down to one grand finale.

"What I'd remembered enjoying about the book was the very human story about faith and friendship and desire and addiction and triumphing over yourself, all of which seemed to me things that the theatre could do so well. I think the emotional impact of our adaptation will be much more personal and real than in the movies. They certainly wowed us with action and spectacle and had really touching moments, but I think the human side of Tolkien's story, the whole Frodo/Sam/Gollum relationship and the Aragorn story and the journeys they make in the show, will make a huge difference to the emotional impact of the evening. If we succeed, I think people will be in tears."

THE OFFICIAL STAGE COMPANION

The MUSIC

Matthew says that what helped him throughout the production was that everyone supported what he wanted to achieve. "I was presented with firm ideas by Kevin and of course from Shaun, Christopher Nightingale and Rob, and so I was trying not to veer from those. For example we looked into a big, expensive, flying effect. We did a test that cost thousands and although it looked good, we realised we weren't doing that sort of production, it didn't fit the ethos. The floor has been another example – making sure that the technology enhances rather than dominates, trying to make aspects of it float rather than be power-driven, which is a formidable task. The key is to hide complexity, hide the technology and therefore keep it within the context of sequences, so that there are, for example, twenty people holding sticks pretending to be Gondor. We worked very hard to keep it all within the one aesthetic and not contradict each other's ideas.

Above Musical Supervisor and Orchestrator Christopher Nightingale.

Opposite Laura Michelle Kelly as Galadriel wearing the new costume created for the London Production.

"Christopher's orchestration has been another manifestation of this, with him trying to make sure we weren't getting too like a traditional musical. Often we found we loved certain songs, or tunes, but we needed to make them sound less familiar, more exotic. I wanted to focus on quirky rather than familiar. There's an integrity that runs through this show that makes it different from other shows. There's a humanity that goes through our Middle-earth, which is reflected in the sets, the clothes, the music and the words. They all combine to mark it out as very different from *The Phantom of the Opera* or *The Lion King*."

Having brought up the fact that this is just as much a musical experience as a straight theatrical one, it seems a good time to

explore this most important aspect of the extravaganza that is *The Lord of the Rings* on stage.

"John Havu was asked to look in Europe," says Kevin, explaining the start of the musical journey this production has taken. "Christopher Nightingale, as musical supervisor and orchestrator, had a very strong feeling that he was going to find what he wanted in A. R. Rahman, with whom he had worked already. He also said that we shouldn't have just one, we should have two composers. He wanted to mix two strong cultural traditions together, so that if Middle-earth was going to have a sound, which was not going to be identified with our world, then the fusing together of these two very different personalities should theoretically produce something that was, by definition, exotic.

KEVIN WALLACE *ON* CHRISTOPHER NIGHTINGALE

Christopher Nightingale falls into the same category as Rob Howell, Peter Darling and Matthew Warchus. They're all people in their thirties, they've come through a certain British social, political, cultural tradition, where they know that the work is what's important, that their talent is what's important, and they don't play status games. So when they're in a room together there's an immediacy to the creative process, which isn't based on politics, it's based on just an instinctive desire to get on and to articulate an approach to the work.

One of the most important meetings was when I put Christopher and Matthew together. They hadn't worked together so I put them into a room and closed the door and they just talked. They talked about the nature of what the music should be for the production, and Matthew was describing the approach he wanted to take and apparently Nightingale said, 'I know exactly what you're talking about, let's go out and buy an album I want you to listen to.' They went out and bought the ironically named *The Black Rider*, a Tom Waits album. What they were interested in was this dark, discordant side of the material, and Matthew said it was exactly what he was thinking of. It demonstrated that Christopher had immediately grasped what Matthew was looking for, that he was on the same wavelength, and that was the beginning of what's become a really successful collaboration.

IT WAS DECIDED TO DIVIDE UP THE WORLD AND START A SEARCH FOR FOLK OR ETHNIC TRADITIONS IN MUSIC OR COMPOSERS WHOSE WORK REFLECTED STRONG TRADITIONAL INFLUENCES.

It was for this reason that John Havu headed to northern Europe to locate the next piece of the musical jigsaw. "During an early meeting with Kevin, Christopher and Matthew," John explains, "a fundamental question was posed: What does music in Middle-earth sound like? Certainly it is most unlikely that it would sound like a modern musical theatre score. What Matthew requested was that the music should be organic, reflecting the environment in which it lives. A second question followed: What does evil music sound like? He wasn't speaking about Hollywood horror movie stuff, rather a music that also sprang naturally from its environment and that was fundamentally disturbing, not just momentarily scary. After this meeting, Christopher and I discussed these fundamental questions. What we were on to was a search for ethnic traditions that could serve as a sound or voice for Middle-earth, something that could be believably identified as coming from this make-believe world.

"In order not to make the assignment too easy on ourselves it was decided to avoid the most obvious tradition of Celtic music, which we viewed as being a cliché. It was decided to divide up the world and start a search for folk or ethnic traditions in music or composers whose work reflected strong traditional influences. Christopher decided he would take a musical trek along the ancient Silk Road from China to India, the Middle East, through the Balkans and on to Spain to see what he could find. As that more mysterious and exotic path was taken, I decided to explore the Ice Road from Iceland, through Scandinavia on to Russia and through Siberia to the Bering Strait.

"Returning home I visited a large music store that had a voluminous section of recordings of folk and world music. After leaving Björk in Iceland, I proceeded through numerous recordings of fiddles and hardangers in Norway and Sweden, all seemingly playing the same melody, along with a few gothic-sounding groups.

Previous The Fellowship is greeted by the Elves of Lothlórien, who sing an uplifting song of welcome during the original Toronto production. For the London production Lothlórien was redesigned and now features new costumes, a new song and a breathtaking aerial display.

I felt I was not getting anywhere and jumped to the Russian section. I had already decided to avoid the standard Russian Orthodox choral tradition as it seemed too easily identifiable and misplaced for *The Lord of the Rings*; I was looking for older traditions. A rather dusty CD caught my eye. It was a field recording of various village choruses in the Mordvinia region of Russia. The opening few bars of the first track struck like lightning. Where was this music from? Was the wrong CD in the jewel case? It sounded like I was in South Africa, but not quite. I could not put my finger on the location or tradition. The women's voices sang with a trumpet-like force in open chords to a sometimes arhythmical pulse. Here was a discovery – the first real clue to a voice for Middle-earth on the Ice Road.

"The liner notes for the recording noted that the Mordvin are an ethnic minority and are linguistically related to the Hungarians and Finns. Being unsure whether Hungary was on Christopher's trek, I retraced my steps to the country I had bypassed, Finland. After listening to a couple of recordings featuring the kantela, a sort of Finnish dulcimer, I came across several CDs by a group called

Below Far from home and under the shadow of Mordor, Frodo and Sam sing of better times.

HERE WE WERE DEALING WITH A SOUND AND THEMES THAT HARKENED BACK TO A PRE-CHRISTIAN EUROPE, A WORLD OF SPELLS, CHANTS, OF DARKNESS AND LIGHT.

Värttinä. The name of the recording was *Ilmatar* (which I later found out was named after the ancient Finnish goddess of air). It is strange to say but after just the first few bars of music I knew I had found what we were looking for. Just as with the recording of the Mordvin village choirs I could not put my finger to a geographical location. I was 'somewhere' where there was a tradition of great strength, powerful, driven, and organic, devoid of musical giveaways as to its origin. European yes, but not influenced by the more obvious traditions. The Finnish language, not being related to any of the major European language groups, added to the feeling of displacement.

"Listening further, I became confident that this group, this sound, was a strong contender to represent the voice of Middle-earth, but what about Matthew's other question regarding evil or dark music? Track 6 of *Ilmatar*, a song entitled 'Äijö', demonstrated that Värttinä was equally up to this task. Here we were dealing with a sound and themes that harkened back to a pre-Christian Europe, a world of spells, chants, of darkness and light.

"Rather excited about this 'discovery' I purchased several recordings and went home and played a section of 'Äijö' over the phone to Christopher back in London. He reacted positively, so it was soon decided to contact the group's manager, Philip Page, who invited us up to Helsinki to meet and join Värttinä on a trip to Estonia where they were playing at the Viljandi folk music festival. Reading Värttinä's web site, it became clear that the ensemble – in various formations – had spent over 20 years delving into the rich tradition of the epic Finnish national poem, the *Kalevala*, for inspiration. On the bus ride back from the festival, guitarist Antto Varilo, who is quite familiar with Tolkien's books, mentioned that Tolkien had studied Finnish. This bit of information and a little research made clear the connection between the Finnish language and Tolkien's own invented languages, and the *Kalevala* and *The Lord of the Rings*. In a way a circle – or ring – had closed. The music of Värttinä drew from one of the primary sources that had provided Tolkien with inspiration for his masterpiece."

This research would prove invaluable; although Kevin Wallace was initially a little concerned that both Rahman and Värttinä might not be accessible enough for a modern audience – he felt that the audience might not actually want to hum the tunes – he became convinced by Christopher and John's belief, and the quality of the music. Kevin explains: "Christopher canvassed for Rahman because he recognised in him somebody who can write a melody that goes right into your bloodstream; but we weren't looking to Rahman to go to his Bollywood tradition, we were looking to him to go to his Indian tradition and also his experience as a classical composer. Meanwhile, John Havu came back with a load of World music from the European arena including *Ilmatar* by Värttinä. They had this very distinctive vocal quality that marked them out. John also played us a CD that probably sells about one copy every two years in some really specialist music shop in Russia – this very exotic vocal tradition, which has moved into the Scandinavian countries. Anyway, this amazing music from Värttinä was the piece that hooked us and made us approach them about joining the project."

According to Christopher, it was the very essence of Tolkien's worldscape that he wanted to capture in the music and themes. His search for this took him from Helsinki in Finland to Chennai in southern India. "My feeling is that the world Tolkien describes is so huge, so vast that it is easy to forget the breadth of it. The book describes, amongst all the European references, Men from the East so I had this vision of Middle-earth as a world that is thousands upon thousands of miles across. Therefore the music needed to reflect that. Why shouldn't there be music that is as exotic to the audience as Chennai was exotic to me?

"I was determined that the music would be contained within the story structure rather than causing a pause. I needed to make sure that the world, the whole story, didn't mysteriously stop when the songs began, which tends to happen in most musicals. So I wanted

to ensure no one was going to be up there singing, 'Oh the Ring is so heavy, I cannot carry it anymore,' while everyone else stopped what they were doing and listened."

"Matthew and I were dead set on finding a distinct, ethnic, musical sound for the story. When I looked back at the books, I was surprised at just how many musical references there are in it – and I believed that to do justice to Tolkien's story, our production needed lots of music. It was quite exciting to create an ethnic sound from scratch, something that had echoes or resonance of music from today and long ago. We went on a search, not knowing what we were looking for but aware – well, all right, hoping – that we'd know it when we found it. I'd worked with Rahman before and so his Bollywood stuff was in my head. He's a wonderful melodist, very chameleonlike; he listens to other peoples' music, draws on it and recreates it in his own unique way.

"Then we went on a search around record shops, listening to World music, taking in things from the Silk Road, gypsy music,

The scene at the Council of Elrond, above which hangs a ball of intricately interwoven branches representing the Elven culture. Underscoring this crucial point in the story the music subtly builds, enhancing the mood of the performance by the original Toronto cast.

THE OFFICIAL STAGE COMPANION

Composer A. R. Rahman, the renowned musician and Bollywood composer, who was brought into the project by Christopher Nightingale.

Bulgarian scores, weird and wonderful bands on obscure record labels. My epiphany was finding Värttinä and their sound: wild, wacky but commercial and easy to listen to. Their music offered enormous heart and soul without being opaque and difficult to appreciate. What was exciting was having a blank canvas, with the freedom to go beyond the obvious. Some people might think *The Lord of the Rings* could have a very Celtic score, but we were immediately thinking of the Scandinavian countries, trying to honour Tolkien's links to Finland, whose vast mythologies and poems he read.

"Anyway, all the roots of northern European music are similar so it might sound Celtic anyway but we didn't want to start there because it was too obvious. Värttinä's music is craggy and bleak, whereas the Celtic tones are much warmer and less primitive. One track, in particular, of Värttinä's, from their album *Ilmatar* – the title of which none of us in England can ever pronounce – 'Äijö', is a crazy thing about an old hag in a woods, during wintertime, who is bitten

The Finnish ensemble Värttinä, the country's most successful folk music group, consisting of: *Susan Aho* – vocals; *Mari Kaasinen* – vocals; *Johanna Virtanen* – vocals; *Janne Lappalainen* – bouzouki, soprano saxophone; *Markku Lepistö* – accordions; *Lassi Logrén* – fiddle, jouhikko; *Jaakko Lukkarinen* – drums, percussion; *Hannu Rantanen* – double bass; *Antto Varilo* – guitars, stringed instruments.

THE LORD OF THE RINGS

by a snake and goes mad. So she starts singing a wild chant and that's where our inspiration started.

"The scary part was our decision to use two diverse artists, and find a way to combine them. But I knew how generous Rahman was, how he loves other peoples' music and how he absorbs things and is inspired by them. So what really interested me was the potential of this crossover, the cross pollination of their two individual styles."

The real challenge was bringing these disparate musical genres under the one umbrella. Finding that first, common link, however, took time as Värttinä composer Janne Lappalainen explains: "When we started composing we didn't know about the other artists involved, such as Rahman, and Shaun McKenna's lyrics, so we just composed our kind of music to the script we had. By the time we went to London and saw Rob Howell's designs and saw how the project would look, we realised the music we had composed was wrong, which meant we had to take a different angle. But just as those designs began shaping our music, we saw ways that our music could shape their design ideas – Rob's models were so inspiring that it meant we could find a way to do our music to suit everyone.

"People wonder if we do World music or Folk music but we don't know the answer," laughs Mari Kaasinen, one of the trio of female harmonisers in Värttinä. "It's just our music, our heart and soul. The only answer we can give is that it's just Värttinä's music; and that whole *Lord of the Rings* concept, it's truly another world and I think Värttinä is good for it – our music suits it."

A. R. Rahman also knew that he could bring something unique to this cross-continental collaboration. "I was so scared when I started scoring all this... until my first piece got okayed by Matthew. Then I knew I could do it, and it got easier once we got right into it. Because of the vision of the whole thing – Rob's, Matthew's, every-one's – musically this had to be quite different from a normal musical; it's trying to take musical theatre in a direction it's never been before."

A screened-off performance booth, where the off-stage singers can watch a monitor to take their cue from the conductor as they provide the soaring musical soundscapes.

THE OFFICIAL STAGE COMPANION

YOU LISTEN TO A PIECE OF MUSIC AND YOU FORGET ABOUT WHO MADE IT OR WHAT THE PROCESS WAS OR WHY THEY COMPOSED IT. YOU ENJOY IT AT THE TIME, YOU JUST LET IT LINGER AND ENJOY IT.

"We bravely tried to marry these two sounds together," says Christopher. "From Värttinä we had their brittle northern European sounds and then we had the luxuriant Indian sounds of Rahman."

And if it seems that, by rights, these two very different approaches to music should not have blended so well, A. R. Rahman explains exactly why, he believes, they did. "There's so much that separates the human race: colour, religion, caste, borders. But a piece of music stands for everyone, it cannot divide the world. You listen to a piece of music and you forget about who made it or what the process was or why they composed it. You enjoy it at the time, you just let it linger and enjoy it."

The music has certainly been a collaboration between very different personalities and talents, but what about the lyrics? Initially, Shaun McKenna and Matthew Warchus tended to rough those out together, although in the long run they found themselves spending more time with the musicians, fitting words to their music. But what was their starting point? After all, in the original work Tolkien supplies a number of songs himself.

"Was I ever tempted to use Tolkien's lyrics?" asks Shaun McKenna. "No, it wouldn't have been appropriate here, and might have taken the music in a direction no one really wanted to go. But then, the music changed a lot during the course of this production. Obviously, I started off working with Stephen Keeling. With Stephen, it's so easy because if I write a lyric, he very rarely changes a word. Värttinä's music doesn't work like that; A. R. Rahman absolutely can't do that. Working with Rahman was like trying to hold water in your hand. It is the most incredibly frustrating process. He likes to have you in the room; he likes you to come up with words but, to give an example, when we sat down to write Galadriel's song, he told me he didn't want any hard consonants, because of the sound of the composition. So, I could use 'ah' and 'oh' and the occasional 'e', 'l' and 'r', but no 't' or 'd'. It's not easy writing a song that says anything with those constraints, but it's a novel challenge.

"It took me a long time to break my habitual writing style before I could really appreciate quite how extraordinary he is. But after a while, by actually sitting in the room with him and watching him build up the music and the sounds and then put the thing together, I realised he really is some kind of genius. And a lovely, lovely man. He's very shy and very gentle: he'd never dream of saying anything to anybody, yet there was a point when he became aware that I was irritated, which then inhibited him from writing any more, so I was firmly told to go with the flow. Once I did that it was fine and it worked. With Keeling, if it takes us three days to write a song that's a long time. The Galadriel song took a year. It was worth it in the end, though, because I think what he came up with is fantastic.

"The Värttinä lyrics, again, were quite hard, because whenever they encountered a problem they would always make something up to sing, in Finnish, but some of it would be nonsense. The challenge for me was that I didn't know what was nonsense and what was Finnish, which caused a couple of hiccups. I'd be working out rhymes and they'd tell me that it wasn't real words they'd been singing. Sometimes bits of it would rhyme and bits of it wouldn't."

"As a group," continues Christopher Nightingale, "Värttinä hadn't done musical theatre, and although Rahman is known for things like *Bombay Dreams*, he's a songwriter and hadn't done this kind of musical arc. I was the glue, keeping their disparate parts together. I didn't want a medley, where you could say 'Oh that's a Värttinä sequence, oh that's Rahman's bit' – it was my job to keep those edges blurred, orchestrate it in such a way that everyone is represented throughout every sequence.

"This kind of massive collaboration – taking in Matthew and Shaun's lyrics as well – is unusual in theatre. And we were so lucky

Frodo unwittingly tempts Galadriel (Rebecca Jackson Mendoza) to take ownership of the Ring. In the original Toronto production Galadriel's costume is decorated with the leaf motif that signifies the Lothlórien Elves and, continuing the tree-theme, her head is crowned with branches.

THE OFFICIAL STAGE COMPANION

– there were no egos, no demarcation separating exactly who did what. It was a genuine collaboration, which is what we wanted and I'm so proud of that; they all provided the raw material, I just joined the dots. If there had been egos getting in the way the score would be very lumpy, as everyone would have had their own personal favourite moments. However, that never happened and as everyone got caught up in the big picture, there was no time for any grandstanding.

"Then, on top of all that, you have the players on the night. The first time we had the orchestra and cast in the same room together and it all meshed was a magical moment. Months of orchestrating for my team, months of rehearsals for the actors and it all just clicked. All that energy and effort was worth it; it paid off and I'm immensely proud of what everyone achieved."

Shaun McKenna picks up the musical journey thread once again. "A significant decision was made early on that we would establish a musical timeline: for example, the Black Riders would use Chaucerian, or Middle English, whereas the Army of the Dead, when they rose, would sing in Old English. With this decided, we then had to find an Anglo-Saxon expert and make sure that it all made grammatical sense. Fortunately we had access to one of the world's finest in Professor Tom Shippey, a highly respected Tolkien scholar and author. Actually, I'm probably the first person ever to have a lyric in Old English in a West End show. So we established this musical timeline, and allocated a period of language to some of the human cultures, but then there was Elvish...

"During my research, I learned that there are people who can speak Elvish, who communicate in Elvish on the internet and who write Elvish poetry. "Before I knew any better, I had imagined that I could make up any old nonsense and no one would be any the wiser. Back then, I believed that the Elvish speakers have picked up some Welsh syntax and grammar, because it seemed the closest, but I now know that there will be plenty of people in the audience who know what Elvish is supposed to sound like. It's all about the case endings, and now I've got books on my shelves about Elvish grammar and the difference between Quenya and Sindarin, because there are two forms of Elvish. In fact, one of our last jobs was to get in a scholar

THE LORD OF THE RINGS

of Tolkien's Elvish languages to check all the grammar and the syntax because we wanted to get it right. Again we were lucky in that we had recommended to us Julian Bradfield, one of the pre-eminent experts in the field.

"Christopher Nightingale deserves a proper composing credit," believes Shaun. "Christopher has a really creative mind, and on this show he has become much more than your usual musical supervisor. He's pulled it all together. Because Matthew and I are writing lyrics, Värttinä are creating vocals and Rahman is producing sounds, we all work in completely different ways, speeds and logics. Christopher became really good at taking a piece, say, of Värttinä's and suggesting that he could lay a small bit of Rahman over it, just to give it an edge. Christopher has constructed the score out of a host of disparate elements and themes. A bit of Värttinä here, a dash of Rahman there, which Christopher will then take back to Värttinä and it's like he's woven the score together, in exactly the organic way that Matthew wanted the whole show to feel."

During a rousing call to arms the warriors of Rohan, as performed by the original Toronto cast, wave the banners of their kingdom.

The DESIGN

T he organic feel to the show is something that has been central to the overall design concept. The man responsible for everything on that level, from the unique, inventive sets to the distinctive costumes, via the outlandish creature designs, is Rob Howell. Rob is softly spoken, unassuming and charmingly self-depreciating about his work, particularly in terms of everything the audience sees during the performance, but this version of *The Lord of the Rings* is an expression of his vision. Although many others have contributed, they all started with Rob's concepts. But where did these mysterious 'concepts' actually come from?

Designer Rob Howell.

"I've known Kevin for maybe ten years. In fact, I knew him before he was with Really Useful but then, like so many of these things, this project just fell out of the sky. I didn't know anything about it; it wasn't a production I knew was on the cards before being approached. The first I knew about it was my agent saying, 'Kevin wants to talk to you… you need to meet Saul Zaentz.'

"My first thought was, I have to admit, that it sounded mad, but at the same time I didn't agree with those people who said it was undoable. It may turn out that our approach isn't the right one, but I refute that it's not doable – I'm struck by the amount of people in my industry who are quite ready to trust that *Henry IV, Part I* and *II* and *Henry V* can be done and yet *The Lord of the Rings* can't be done. So, I was certainly daunted but I was also excited by the challenge. At no point did I ever believe it was impossible."

So, how exactly does one go about getting inspiration for a project this vast without, as Rob is proud to say, having watched any of the Peter Jackson movies, to avoid comparisons? And this was despite valiant attempts by his children to make him do so "because they're great fans, and always seem to be watching one of them". Without that most obvious of inspirations, was it back to the book or something more specific?

"I had my 'Eureka' moment one weekend down in Cornwall. At the Eden Project, in fact. I was wandering around, the production weighing heavily on my mind, and I knew that I wanted natural textures – going by the books, this seemed to be a prerequisite – but I had no idea what the environment, the holding space for the events on stage, was going to be. And then there in front of me was this amazing onion-shaped folly, woven out of cane; as you walked into it you looked up from below, through these oval-shaped windows, into the pinnacle. Through these windows, I could see little stickmen hanging on string from what looked to be like fishing rods coming out of the top of the onion. And very quickly it was easy to imagine

KEVIN WALLACE *ON* ROB HOWELL

I had worked with Rob Howell on two previous occasions. I saw him as the designer of his generation, who was clearly following in the footsteps of the great designers who'd gone before in the first phase of our large-scale musical theatre, the Seventies and Eighties surge of British musicals – Napier and Björnsen, in particular, those two great designers. Rob was the new pretender, and had demonstrated that in a revival of *Sunset Boulevard* that we did on tour in the UK; there was also his extraordinary designs for *Sophie's Choice* at the Opera House. This was somebody who could design on a grand scale and yet was sensitive to, in a piece of musical theatre, the need for the action to continue. You don't have blackouts in Rob Howell productions, you move on, and that's an essential of musical theatre – of getting and keeping the ball in the air all evening. So, I talked to Matthew and Rob about the marriage of Matthew's direction and Rob's design and ensured that that was something that was going to work. In fact they had worked together before, so I already knew it'd be fine.

THE OFFICIAL STAGE COMPANION

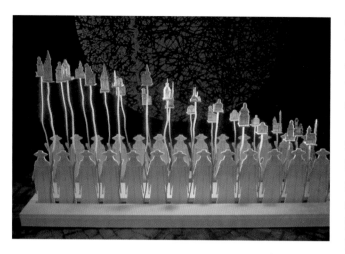

As with most of the key design elements, Rob Howell and his team built a model of the Gondorian people which could be placed into Rob's model of the stage so that each element could be tailored to be as visually impactful as possible.

that all of this woven texture could be a vertical surface in a theatre; it could be a cloth or a wall, and through it you'd see somebody or some thing.

"These little stickmen were inspirational. If they'd been plastic dolls, it wouldn't have had such a resonance, but a little crudely bound stickman on a bit of string was strikingly low-tech and utterly charming. Immediately I got a sense of this root structure that could be wrapped around and you'd see through it. I knew then that I had envisioned the staging space that the audience are with throughout the whole evening. It needed to have an energy to it that was exciting and frightening and full of texture and identity. And this thing just jumped out as something that could be that."

Matthew Warchus is full of praise for Rob's work on the show: "From our earliest conversations, I discovered that Rob and I shared the same tastes and understanding of the book. When we'd read it, we were both of one mind regarding the design, the look of the show. It was all there. The principles, the idea of it all being derived from the natural world are themes of the show that are entirely in keeping with the book. For example, I remember a phone call in which Rob talked about making the stage circular – I needed no convincing of that, it just seemed obvious. I then suggested that it would be great if we could get that stage both revolving and lifting, changing shape, and so we talked a lot about fairground rides, the Giant's Causeway in Ireland with its different-sized stones and how we

WHEN WE'D READ IT, WE WERE BOTH OF ONE MIND REGARDING THE DESIGN, THE LOOK OF THE SHOW. IT WAS ALL THERE. THE PRINCIPLES, THE IDEA OF IT ALL BEING DERIVED FROM THE NATURAL WORLD ARE THEMES OF THE SHOW THAT ARE ENTIRELY IN KEEPING WITH THE BOOK.

could get the stage to replicate these things. We talked about all that together and even decided between us that the flooring should be the rings of a tree. This whole period was a total meeting of minds: one of us would say something, the other replied, 'Yes, and...' and we'd keep developing our ideas from there. I don't remember ever saying no, because we were striving for the same thing.

"After all this, the longer discussions and debates that followed were about filling in the gaps, about how much scenery there needed to be in Bree or did we need walls for Orthanc, and so on. We needed to ensure that the audience got a lot a treats for their money. With this in mind, we were now asking important and commercially relevant questions: Would people get the thrills they deserved? Would we deliver evocative worlds with genuinely magical characters? So we wanted the environments to be organic, to involve the audience, quite literally at times as some of them extend into the auditorium. Certain parts of the design process happened instantaneously, others took years, just tweaking or rethinking things that we believed we'd

To show the scale of the Gondorian city, each actor from the original Toronto cast carries a tiny dwelling on variously sized poles to give both a sense of depth of vision and the scope of the city of Gondor.

THE OFFICIAL STAGE COMPANION

Opposite The banner
of Saruman's Orcs
(Colin Heath and Peter
van Gestel) features
the distinctive white
hand of the wizard,
which Tolkien wrote
about in the book.

solved until we realised they couldn't be afforded. It's been a muscular process designing this show, fluid, and involving everyone and everything. But it all started with Rob's trip to the Eden Project."

"I was pleased that both Kevin and Matthew seemed to be immediately receptive to this rather nebulous idea," Rob says. "It's a texture that will light in so many different ways and provide a really edgy cradle for the story – something that's got more lift and spirit to it than traditional theatres. Also, it will represent great value in that we can reuse it to fuel the space with a different charge and energy. I think the thing is that, if we get it right, it'll feel like a root system. What the root system's doing is sending a message to the audience that this story has been going for thousands and thousands of years. We're not looking at a young plant here, we're looking at enormous roots that are black and twisted and grown round each other and yet what's shooting out into the auditorium still seems to be growing. It's not lush and fresh, it's a twisted, darkened version of organic life; I hope that it suggests there's a history to it, which seems to be completely out of scale with our understanding of life and history. It should be like a small piece of the timeline in the continuing history of Middle-earth, which is ongoing. The audience should feel they're joining something – they're not there at the start of the story, or at the end of it; they're here for this part of the timeline. And if we get it right, that's what will come across."

Right While searching
for inspiration for the
overall design of the
show, Rob Howell
visited the Eden
Project in Cornwall.
One of the cane
structures there was
to prove instrumental
in shaping the idea of
interwoven branches
that could be used
as vertical structures,
which both screened
parts of the stage
and also allowed
the audience to see
events unfolding
through them.

The STAGE

Whilst the organic look and feel permeates much of Rob's work on *The Lord of the Rings*, there's the dichotomy of modern technical wizardry, be it the seventeen-lift floor, the metal sculptures that represent the flowering emergence of Lothlórien or the dangerous, spiky, wholly unnatural Orc armour and weaponry. So how does Rob, while creating the delicacy of the plant-like stage, balance that in his mind with the needs of the technical marvels that will actually help the story unfold?

"It's a bit of a challenge, really, for myself and the poor souls who have to make it all work without sacrificing the look and feel of the show. As a designer, a lot of what I and my team do is physics. If you put something 'here', then there isn't room for something else 'there'. So, it's making sure that I'm not being irresponsible by

Peter Darling and his team get used to the way the elevating stage will work during practice sessions in the Toronto rehearsal studio.

overcrowding the space of the stage's environment and expecting things to live in the same place, when clearly they can't, and understanding that if I devote a lot of space to one thing, then other things will suffer because there's going to be a knock-on effect. As long as I know I'm being responsible about the space, and that physics should allow this thing to move in this way, then I feel okay about saying to an engineer: 'I don't know how on earth this is going to be done' – because I don't know anything about inverters and motors and they do! That's what they love and they have, obviously, risen to the challenge for this show.

"In itself, there's nothing remarkable about what we're doing with our stage because everyone's seen a stage lift up before, everybody's seen one revolve before, everybody's seen three revolves going in opposite directions, and so on. What's remarkable with ours is the quantity, and I can quite happily say that there's going to be seventeen lifts on the stage.

"The stage is probably the most important thing we've done. I know that sounds obvious, but it truly is because it's there for the

With each of the stage's seventeen sections moving up and down to create a cleverly shifting landscape, and the whole thing revolving, the battle of Helm's Deep is a truly complex scene to choreograph and perform.

These three images demonstrate how fabric netting would be used to replicate the idea of water on the Ford of Bruinen, where water-horses emerge to wash the pursuing Black Riders away from Frodo and the hobbits. First appearing as panels to comprise a flat screen, with images projected on to them, they would be twisted together as the panels rotate around the circular stage to form a cone, swallowing the Riders who disappear as the cone flattens to the floor.

whole three hours, that basic shape and silhouette. No scene changes, no blackouts, no curtains coming own. It functions the whole time. There's a very familiar technique to staging, to story-telling on a stage, where you do something called a front cloth. That means where you perform a scene in front of another piece of stuff. Meanwhile, upstage of that, behind the cloth, you're changing the scenery in some way and then for no apparent reason that you can justify, other than we accept it, seemingly the hand of God takes away the front cloth and we're in another place. Everybody does this, but it didn't seem to me that this story should be told using that technique because you want to understand and witness the forces that are at work to shift the landscape.

"We've chosen a harder journey, which is to show every change; you see everything happen, so there's constancy to that journey and there's constancy to the space, which suits my aesthetic, my tastes. That's not the only reason for doing it, but there's something about a journey in which, in real terms, you don't actually go anywhere. You've got this massive journey which the Fellowship undertake, you take everybody with you, but in the end the hotspot for any event we witness is the centre of the stage. To take any character on a journey, in any story, you take them out of that central area and then you need to bring them back. They actually haven't gone anywhere – but obviously the revolve helps us achieve this, and the lifts help us take people to somewhere within that triangle.

"If the audience accepts and acknowledges all of Middle-earth's realities, and the events of the story, then we don't want to have to take people off stage or out of sight in order to join them at the next stage of their journey. If we did this, it would be heading towards the insanity of the other, traditional way of staging it. Are we really going to bring on another cloth, another scenic gesture, for every part of this journey? Or is that just futile and exhausting, and runs the risk of breaking the mood, forcing the audience to say, 'Oh, come on, if I have to see another thing fly in, I'm going to scream'?

"It seemed to be that when we meet Shelob or an Ent or something else unique to Middle-earth, as long as the holding space seems to be right, and has the energy for all the different places you're going, then that's money in the bank for every scene. It lightens the load of the production and it means you're sharing a shorthand with the audience, and trusting them that they can make the journey with Frodo, Sam and the others without having to have everything spelled out. After all, the last thing you want to do is exhaust them with a futile attempt to recreate the depth of the book, because then we're doing New Line's film. And that is not celebrating what theatre does best. When theatre is at its best, it's trusting an audience and sharing with them. It's saying, 'Come with

Overleaf Rohan warriors from the original Toronto cast, led by Aragorn, Legolas and Gimli, salute the audience.

TO TAKE ANY CHARACTER ON A JOURNEY, IN ANY STORY, YOU TAKE THEM OUT OF THAT CENTRAL AREA AND THEN YOU NEED TO BRING THEM BACK. THEY ACTUALLY HAVEN'T GONE ANYWHERE – BUT OBVIOUSLY THE REVOLVE HELPS US ACHIEVE THIS, AND THE LIFTS HELP US TAKE PEOPLE TO SOMEWHERE WITHIN THAT TRIANGLE.

87

us on this journey, fill in the gaps in this story yourself but don't worry, we're holding your hand.' We're trying to celebrate what theatre does best, and the revolving, lifting stage is the best way to create that.

"We've got a great team, particularly those who have worked on the stage itself, from Delstar. Every time we came across something I wanted to do that they weren't sure how to achieve, rather than throwing up their hands in horror, they had a high enough level of confidence so that they always said that anything should be possible. We're not breaking new ground here, that would be too lofty a claim, but it is stuff that nobody's actually tried before in this format. I suppose the closest we got to breaking new ground was the floor. With so many lifts and the size of it, the time needed to build it, it was unlikely we were

ever going to have it in rehearsals. In actual fact, it turned out we did indeed have it for a couple of weeks, but it was still not enough time for the company to learn how to fully use it. However, it gave us some necessary practice time, to see what would and wouldn't work when you're moving across a constantly changing, revolving landscape. Occasionally, it's frightening and scary and you get lost and end up on the wrong side of the stage in a battle, with the wrong person, and more time would have shown us earlier how we were going to help them through all of that. But people cope.

"One novelty was working with Ralph Goyarts at Silicon Scenery to develop software for the computers in my studio. We wanted it to work in such a way that we could create a timeline for each of the lifts to the millimetre, and to the second. That timeline could then be exported and make sense to the computers at Delstar, so we could programme six minutes' worth of Helm's Deep sequence, months ahead of when we would be working on this complex battle sequence. We could all then sit down and look at it as a fully rendered animation in my studio, before programming it into the floor. That way we knew every tiny movement needed to make and speed up the trial and

Some sets are intricate, others are achieved through simple placements of organic-looking structures. For the scenes at Moria (*opposite*) in the original Toronto production, the vast subterranean kingdom of the Dwarves, frameworks of jagged metal were constructed to give the appearance of giant pillars of stone. The tubular frames (*above*) were linked with chain so that they could be quickly extended and collapsed to keep pace with the fast-moving events of the story.

THE OFFICIAL STAGE COMPANION

With the framework for the Balrog installed and the stage in position, work progresses on programming the lighting for maximum impact during what is one of the show's most memorable scenes. For the arrival of the "creature of shadow and flame" a stark white curtain of light and smoke will project the dark shape forward on to the audience.

error process; otherwise you would lose huge amounts of precious time with automation, waiting hours and hours, days, weeks probably, to automate the full-size stage for real with that many moving parts, for just six minutes' worth of sequence. So, for us to be able to do all of that, and get a sense of whether we liked the shape of something in my studio before committing to the full-size stage – it was terribly novel. I'm not sure that's been done on this scale before.

"The use of computers, in our case Apple Macs using Cinema-4D with specially written plug-ins for those who want to know, is becoming more commonplace, but when I was at college stage plans were pieces of paper in sections, and that's what you'd get through the post, rolled up in a tube, when you started a job. Now, of course, everything's emailed because it's all done digitally and so it's unthinkable now for any theatre designer not to be computer literate. It's strange; it's brought about a different way of working. With paper stage plans, you can literally look from above and see everything at

THE LORD OF THE RINGS

the same time. Digitally, unless you've got an enormous monitor, or you're working in a tiny scale, it's very difficult to do that. So there is a sense of loss from my generation, but I imagine there won't be from the next because that's how they have always worked.

"To me, there's something fantastic about an unsharpened pencil scratching round on a big paper drawing. That's where big sweeping ideas happen, whereas because of the deadly accuracy of the computer everything is more instant, less conceptual. Less instinctive, perhaps. The computer, I think, is able to oblige us to be more accurate than we need – does it matter when it tells us that the line is 57.8 millimetres long? You didn't care when it was drawn with a pencil, but none of that preparatory work's done on the computer these days. Your first idea on the computer feels final because it's neat: it's got a border, and it's got a box around it, everything's tidy. It's tidy too quickly. Of course, computers give us a more overall view, a chance to see everything from a variety of angles, including the audiences, and with the programming we've

Above The model of Bag End, showing the original design. For the finished design (*below* featuring James Loye and Brent Carver) the three elements of door, window and fire were retained and seamlessly linked by extending the circular frame of the door.

In the original Toronto production, during the scene where Aragorn challenges the elderly King Théoden and his niece Éowyn to stand up to Saruman's Orc army, the Rohan symbol of a white horse is projected on to a screen at the back. Simple spot-lighting creates an arresting triptych, with the horse symbolising all that is at stake.

got it's intelligent in a way so that it understands foreshortening and can calculate all those complex sums for you. So what we're seeing on screen is a true representation of what the audience will see when sat in the theatre.

"Despite my fondness for pencil sketches, I didn't do too much on paper for *The Lord of the Rings*. Sometimes, a rough is just a doodle on the corner of a bit of paper, and that becomes an idea that becomes a model and the model gets drawn up straight away on computer. It's strange, because on a show like this I think it will seem wrong to the audience if everything feels millimetre perfect. But of course it is, or will have to be. Obviously, there are some shows where it would be good to feel millimetre perfect, but we're going for rough,

SOMETIMES, A ROUGH IS JUST A DOODLE ON THE CORNER OF A BIT OF PAPER, AND THAT BECOMES AN IDEA THAT BECOMES A MODEL AND THE MODEL GETS DRAWN UP STRAIGHT AWAY ON COMPUTER.

THE LORD OF THE RINGS

coarse looks and if everything is neat and ordered, you can't help but lose that organic feeling of hand-made sets, costumes and props.

"The design for this project," Rob continues, "is a journey, and the easy trap to fall into is to forget the source material and just treat it as a new thing, ignoring what Tolkien established. To take the journey metaphor further, we want to feel as if there are different cultures brought in with each act of the play, different influences, moods, textures, climate and temperature, all created using organic materials rather than man-made ones.

"I really feel that, just because the Mines of Moria have a particular look and the pillars are treated in a certain way, it shouldn't give you any clue at all as to what's going to come up out of the floor. Similarly, just because the Black Riders are created the way that they are, I don't want the audience to assume that the Balrog's going to be designed the same way, or operated in the same manner, so we're constantly trying to throw people off the scent. To fool them and say, 'You weren't expecting that, were you?'"

Frodo (James Loye) recovers from his ordeal in a bedroom in Elrond's haven at Rivendell. The ball that hung over the Council scene is repeated in miniature on the bedposts and staves of the guardians. The Moon, a further circular device to frame the scene, looks down on the night-time visit of Arwen (Carly Street).

THE OFFICIAL STAGE COMPANION

The BALROG

Hand-made rather than machine built is very much the order of the day – and nowhere is that more obvious than in the aforementioned creature that rules the Mines of Moria, the Balrog. Rob had very definite ideas of how he wanted the Balrog to look, or rather how it should not look – no technology, nothing artificial, which is right for such a primal creature. Instead, he turned to two outside contractors, Carl Robertshaw of the Kite Studio for the construction materials and Dave Brill of the British Origami Society for the actual creation of the creature.

"I received a call in March 2004 from Kevin Wallace's office asking if I wanted to get involved," Dave explains. "Rob Howell had seen pictures of some of my work on the BOS website and thought I might be a suitable candidate for helping to design the Balrog figure. This was because he wanted it to have an origami basis and feel. I had a chat on the phone and later a meeting with him: it sounded challenging and so I said I'd do what I could. Over the following months, we had lots more discussions and meetings down at Rob's studio, and later at Carl Robertshaw's studios where eventually a small-scale version of the Balrog was finalised. It was really a three-way design partnership between Rob, Carl and me. We've all had pretty equal input into the design and for me it was a really stimulating experience working with these two guys who are at the top of their very different creative trees, although it was Carl who then worked on building the full-scale version."

An early pass at the origami-based Balrog, complete with scorch marks to reproduce its flaming skin and a small figure for scale, is placed on Rob's model of the stage.

THE LORD OF THE RINGS

The full-sized creature is placed on its metal frame. During the show it will rise out of the centre of the stage, its wings unfurling. The ravages of its ancient existence are evident in the burned and tattered fabric.

"Rob contacted me to explore the creation of the Balrog. He came to the studio and started talking kites and origami!" is Carl's recollection. "I couldn't resist getting involved in this project because it's such a big challenge and something I've never done before. My business is my passion (some might say obsession) for making kites. I've flown sport kites competitively for ten years and I've always made kites and other things like lampshades, flags and screens. The demand has grown for what I do, and seven years ago I decided to turn it into a full-time business. I've made set pieces for stage theatre before, because of my background. Now we get enquiries from all over the world for kites and some weird and strange projects – just like this one. *The Lord of the Rings* is one of those 'once in a lifetime' opportunities and influenced by Rob's design and Dave's origami sculptures – their vision of the Balrog – meant that I created the creature by mixing inflatable and tensioned structures with a mechanized frame. Seeing the work taking shape in the studio is an inspiration to the scale of the whole job. The textures and effect that we were after with the fabrics was unique, and I would not have ended up at this result by myself – Rob's vision pushed us to make something that goes way beyond our usual experiences."

THE OFFICIAL STAGE COMPANION

The ENTS

Opposite The Ents, performed by the original Toronto cast, are enhanced by the projection of leaves across the stage to convey that we are deep in their forest home of Fangorn.

Below Merry and Pippin do not know whether Treebeard is friend or foe.

Whereas Tolkien's own description of the Balrog is vague and open to interpretation, he was considerably more specific about the inhabitants of Fangorn Forest, the tree-like Ents. If you have a multimillion-dollar budget and unlimited computer-generated imagery on screen, walking, talking trees are a doddle. On stage, they could easily end up looking more akin to a terrible end-of-pier pantomime put on by a class of eight-year-olds. It's a tricky line to tread, and Rob Howell agrees:

"The Ents are a huge trap waiting for you to fall into. The thing is, Tolkien absolutely adored trees, which is clear from the pain

and the melancholy he describes in the book whenever trees are being chopped down and burnt. It's a huge thing for him. So, number one, we had to take the Ents seriously as a theatre gesture and not render them as a hokey cop-out. They had to be an event within our story in the same way they're an emotional event for Tolkien. You have to give them proper weight. So there's something shifty and depressing and a bit of cheat to just use technology and fabricated materials for that kind of event.

"We decided that we wanted to use human beings, actors or movement people with circus skills. Obviously the Ents are trees, or tree-like, and trees are taller than men so we hit upon the solution of men on stilts. But we were still faced with the conundrum of the precise treatment of that idea; how do we make them feel plausible?

Above A performer rehearses walking like an Ent. Because of the extreme height of the stilts safety is of paramount importance, so the Ents are each given a staff to create a third point of balance and the performers are harnessed so that if they were to fall they would be caught before reaching the ground.

For me, it's the balancing act between man and tree – are we saying these are trees that look a bit like human beings or are they human beings who look a bit like trees? So we took the approach that they should be these wonderful, countryside grandfathers with old cardigans and soft-felt hats and fingerless gloves – it should be like meeting a shepherd in a forest. When we thought of it in that way, it was a huge relief in respect of what they were going to be wearing, as it became a costume rather than a creature – and that in turn seemed to justify that they're performers on three-metre stilts, rather than dodgy tree costumes.

"WE DECIDED THAT WE WANTED TO USE HUMAN BEINGS, ACTORS OR MOVEMENT PEOPLE WITH CIRCUS SKILLS.

"There'll be an amazing charge coming off the stage when twelve performers on these incredibly tall stilts – very tall even for stilt-walkers – are all there. It will have the emotional weight we want, and it'll be a moment that should acknowledge how special trees were for Tolkien and how special they are to the story. Of course, we could have gone more traditional, almost Disney-like, and depicted living trees but I prefer our approach. This world we've created as our take on *The Lord of the Rings* is not a shiny, plastic pop-culture thing. It's organic and real. I would understand if someone was turning up, expecting that but ultimately I think what they're going to get will be so much more rewarding and enjoyable on so many different levels. From admiring the sheer skill of people up there, performing at such height, to feeling the warmth that you have when you've spent time with wise, older people. It's fitting that they have that place in the story. So, I'm no more worried about people turning up with a misconception about the Ents than I would them having a misconception about anything else we're doing. As long as we're replacing what they're expecting with something worthwhile, that's great. It's a surprise: I hope they go away thinking that what they saw wasn't what they were expecting, but it was still great."

Left An early conceptual drawing of one of the Ents. The look proved so successful that almost nothing was changed when creating the final costume (*right*).

Right The hobbits Merry (Richard Henders) and Pippin (Owen Sharpe) are dwarfed by the towering presence of Treebeard (Michael Hobbs), whose costume resembles that of an old farmer and whose grey beard extends downwards to become a mossy thatch.

The GREEN LIGHT

S o while all this was going on, being planned and prepared, Kevin Wallace, having brought his team together, was still waiting for a yes or no from Saul Zaentz's people in America.

"After the meeting in Saul's office in Berkeley in early 2003, I went to lunch with Al Bendich and Frank Noonan. We lunched, we talked about politics, art, sport, everything. We also talked a bit about *The Lord of the Rings*, and there was a degree of bonding that took place during that meeting. As I left them they said, 'Okay, look. We're going to talk to Saul and we will get back to you really quickly.' I got back at about six o'clock in the evening and my partner, William, had been hanging out at the hotel all day. But he didn't mind because he thought the longer I was away, the better he believed my day must have gone – he said that if I'd got back in half an hour, it would have been a pretty ropey meeting. So I felt really confident that it was going to come through.

"We flew back to London and a couple of days later I got a phone call from Laurie to say that Saul had confirmed that they were going to do the deal. From then on, I did the commercial negotiations myself with Norman Rudman representing Saul, and then I'd go back and talk to my lawyer, David Wills, about the legal stuff that was coming up during the day, and Norman would go back to Al. This continued for ten weeks, and then we set a date. It was clear that we were going to get it signed, so I said I was going to assume the deal would be done by 15 April. I then made an appointment to see Dewynters, who would be the marketing agency for the production, and along with Peter Thompson, who at a second meeting agreed to be the press rep, we'd work toward that deadline, just move heaven and earth to get it done. The night before the meetings, at two in the morning, the fax machine buzzed into life and woke me up. I went upstairs and it was a fax from Norman saying he was delighted to confirm that the deal memo had been signed, and that it would be coming through shortly. Forty-five minutes later I got up again because the fax machine started to buzz and these twenty-two pages came through, initialled, and the twenty-second page was the one that had the signatures from Saul Zaentz and Tolkien Enterprises. When that page came off the fax machine, it represented the culmination of the first phase of the project and eighteen months of hard work. We celebrated with a good Irish whiskey that night!

"The next challenge was getting the creative team into a room together. So we decided that, for the first week of May 2003, we were going to bring together Matthew and Christopher and Rob, John Havu, myself, Laurie Battle over from the States, Shaun and Bernd Stromberger and Stephen Keeling. We met for a number of days to go through the material, and to have conversations. Matthew said some things that I've never forgotten, and which have totally influenced the work of the composers and the designers and indeed of himself and Shaun and the text. He talked about the fact that musical theatre today, for the contemporary audience, essentially means *The Producers*, *The Full Monty*, *Hairspray*, *Mamma Mia!*: all

In the original Toronto production Galadriel (Rebecca Jackson Mendoza), Elrond (Victor A. Young) and Arwen (Carly Street) magically observe events from afar, the actors are placed at the back of the stage. The Ring surrounds them, so they are able to observe but not influence the fate of the Fellowship. This scene would be cut for the London production.

THE OFFICIAL STAGE COMPANION

The character of Gollum (Michael Therriault) is of key importance to the whole story. Although it is easy to see him as a monster and one of the villains of the piece he is also a tragic victim, and Frodo's pity for Gollum will prove decisive in influencing the outcome of the Fellowship's quest.

pieces of theatre that have a nod and a wink to the audience, which have a degree of irony, sarcasm and self-deprecating wit. Matthew firmly believed that, if one was going to bring *The Lord of the Rings* to the stage, you had to do so with the same integrity and intensity as if you were doing the Mystery Plays – with a passion. The audience had to believe in the power of the Ring, they had to be completely imaginatively and emotionally enthralled, there had to be that total suspension of disbelief. The audience had to be as engaged in the process as Shakespeare's first audiences would have been, therefore completely different to what people were actually used to seeing in 2003 in large-scale commercial shows.

"Trying to find the language for the production, Matthew's references were the story-telling techniques used by Trevor Nunn, when he did *Nicholas Nickleby* at the RSC that Matthew and I and most of the creative team would have seen. And he was talking about the use of poor theatre and street theatre in design that was drawn upon by

Shockheaded Peter. The release of the imagination through visual spectacle of both *Cirque du Soleil* and *The Lion King*, and the fact that a great text can be brought to life by fine actors but a density and richness of language was going to be essential to the piece as well. It had to be that good, because Tolkien was that good. He was taking the most appropriate elements of theatre tradition, and applying them to *The Lord of the Rings*, as opposed to taking *The Lord of the Rings* and trying to squeeze it and fashion it into a particular, traditional musical theatre.

"Matthew started to work closely with Shaun in redrafting the script to that brief. We then decided that we would do a test on some of the existing music to see if this could respond to Matthew's brief. It was not an unsatisfactory response, but it wasn't ultimately what he wanted – he had talked about the material having an integrity, an antiquity... it needed to have credibility on stage so the audience were really going to say, 'I believe'.

"The conclusion that we reached was that it was actually unfair to Keeling and Stromberger. They had written a score, which was their response to *The Lord of the Rings*, and which was a more traditional response than that which Matthew was after. I had to have some very difficult conversations with Stephen and Bernd, because they had put in an enormous amount of work getting us to this point; I asked them to step back from the project, which they both very graciously did. We then needed to find composers who, using their own cultural traditions and unique musicality, could actually fulfil the brief that Matthew had imagined and that he and Christopher had consolidated and articulated. Ultimately our search led us to A. R. Rahman and Värttinä, but we also needed to bring in other experts in their respective fields to help us create the world we were striving to find."

THE AUDIENCE HAD TO BE AS ENGAGED IN THE PROCESS AS SHAKESPEARE'S FIRST AUDIENCES WOULD HAVE BEEN, THEREFORE COMPLETELY DIFFERENT TO WHAT PEOPLE WERE ACTUALLY USED TO SEEING IN 2003 IN LARGE-SCALE COMMERCIAL SHOWS.

THE OFFICIAL STAGE COMPANION

ATTENTION ALL
PLEASE DO NOT
TOUCH ANY
BUTTONS OR
SWITCHES THAT
YOU HAVEN'T
INSTALLED
YOURSELF!

The PERFORMANCE

One area of expertise that needed to be explored in some depth was performance. With songs, fights and bizarre creatures, it was clear this wasn't a traditional acting job for anyone who was lucky enough to be cast. This cross-pollination of actors, singers, performers and circus-trained artists fell under the responsibility of choreographer Peter Darling, his associate choreographer Rob Tannion, and the circus skills specialist, Alex Frith. Peter explains how he joined the production:

"I'd worked with Matthew on *Our House* and it'd been a real fun and amicable working environment. Often the whole collaboration between choreographer and director is a difficult one because you're dipping into each other's work, and so I think when it goes well it's something that you want to repeat. Matthew said that he was doing *The Lord of the Rings*, and did I want to do it? At the time, I'd been doing auditions and workshops for *Billy Elliot* and I'd asked Rob Tannion if he might be available to do *Billy*, but he wasn't. So when this came up I thought that it'd be perfect, if Rob wanted to be the associate choreographer on it."

Rob nods enthusiastically: "I jumped in; and because Peter asked me so far ahead, I had time to re-plan other things that had been arranged. We actually have very different backgrounds, as I trained mainly through dance, and have worked as a dancer for a long time. But I have other interests – studying martial arts and working with fight choreography as well. Although at the end of the day it is Peter's artistic vision that will take things through, I have plenty of things I can bring to the table and offer up as well as being inspired by and getting feedback from him."

Above Choreographer Peter Darling.

Opposite Many hours of practice went into ensuring that the fight scenes looked authentic and exciting, yet posed no real danger to the performers of the original Toronto cast.

THE OFFICIAL STAGE COMPANION

KEVIN WALLACE *ON* PETER DARLING

I'd worked with Peter Darling before – and fortunately so had Matthew and Rob Howell – on two productions, on the revival of *Sunset Boulevard*, and also on a small-scale production, *Closer to Heaven*, the Pet Shop Boys musical. So we knew each other and I knew Peter's tradition comes out of physical theatre and his movement comes out of situation and out of character, and his having being an actor – he's not a straight-forward "song-and-dance choreographer", or a "*42nd Street* choreographer". His work on *Billy Elliot* demonstrates the ingenuity of his work – one critic drew a comparison between the work of *West Side Story*, and what Darling has done in *Billy Elliot*, and when you see it, you see that his work in Stephen Daldrey's production elevates the whole show, taking it to a different level. I'm a huge fan of Peter's work, and really respect him, and again he is obsessed with what he does. He has this rigorous, obsessive approach to the work, which at this level you have to have. But he also has a wit and sense of humour and he's a guy in his thirties, like Matthew and Rob, so there is a healthy lack of destructive ego in the group.

"I'm the one who's always going to make the executive decision," Peter explains, "and ultimately it's my vision for the sequences. Then Rob, with his wealth of other knowledge that I don't have, brings a lot of it to life. The difference with this show is that on previous ones I map out all the material beforehand because you're dealing with a clearer set-up. For instance, on *Billy Elliot* they're going to do a form of ballet or a form of tap, and those styles are ones that I am accustomed to working in. Whereas on *The Lord of the Rings*, we're looking to take types of movement and dance that will have been seen before, but turn them on their head. So, say I have this notion that in the last battle the floor will be exploding with bodies, as if the floor is pushing the bodies up: Rob and I will therefore explore new kinds of movements, for instance bouncing, and see just how many different ways the human body can bounce.

"A lot of it's task-based," adds Rob. "In a pre-defined dance form, such as ballet or even tap, there's a repertoire of movement; there's a

THE LORD OF THE RINGS

certain formula and the interest comes out of how you arrange it – that's the joy of choreography. Here, however, it's about using a multitude of different forms, mixing them up, maybe using contact improvisation or partnering work, where that's not necessarily a form that's often used in the traditional discipline of theatre. We're very keen to find areas of movement that are not common to mainstream theatre work."

Peter concurs: "Indeed, the first thing I thought when Kevin Wallace asked me to become involved was that there wasn't really going to be much for me to do as a choreographer... then I started to realise that actually it would all be movement, but in a way that hopefully won't be obvious. I hoped that we could find people who would gain an understanding of how their species move, and that's when I started to think fights could be more than *ka-chink*, *ka-chink*, *ka-chink* and actually be a world that could incorporate some of the language that Rob and I have acquired or learned or understood over the years."

"The first question I wanted answered," says Rob, "was: 'Is it one book or is it going to be all three? And how are we going to do it in a stage performance?' Then I read the script and Peter and I started working out answers to those questions. We had a couple of what we call research-and-development periods, where we started looking at how the hobbits would move, what sort of dance would be a dance that is related to a hobbit. How would some of the Elves walk? What do the Orcs move like? I've practiced a lot of movements using objects or props or set and furniture as part of the choreographic form, so although I hadn't necessarily worked before with, for example, the crutches the Orcs use, one of the good things about a prop is that, yes, they're limiting but you can use that limitation as a positive – it can inform the movement content."

WE'RE VERY KEEN TO FIND AREAS OF MOVEMENT THAT ARE NOT COMMON TO MAINSTREAM THEATRE WORK.

THE OFFICIAL STAGE COMPANION

The WEAPONRY & PROPS

"Props are fine," adds Peter. "I use them all the time because I think they provoke different movements to the ones you may have initially come up with; they force you to compromise, to look at everything differently, which I think is great. It adds to the challenge and stops it becoming just another set of movements you've choreographed a hundred times before. Of course, it can be a difficult compromise but it's one that has to be found between functionality and its look. We have had Orc crutches that have looked amazing, but they're unwieldy and you just know that they're going to cause terrible repetitive-arm syndrome. So, we went back and forth with Simon Brindle at Artisan Armours, who were making these things, to get something that fitted the ethic of his and Rob Howell's designs but were still practical for the performers. Specifically with the crutches, the final version was version seven – Simon's team made seven different prototypes, all of which were brought along, all of which were tried out."

"And I was there each time," adds Rob, "saying: 'Yes, that's great... Oh, wow, if the blade was like this... Actually, oh, no, you know I said have the blade like that? Actually every time I try and do this, it touches here or it's far too heavy...' The truth is that the crutch we now have is a tiny bit heavier than we'd really like but we can manage, and that's the important thing."

As Peter mentions above, Simon Brindle and his company, Artisan Armours, supplied the suits of armour, the weapons and prosthetics for the production. Being the designer, was Rob Howell responsible for bringing Simon onboard?

Opposite Gimli (Sévan Stephan) shows off his full costume and weapons. Rob Howell wanted the runic emblems to represent medals or talismans from different Dwarvish conquests, and these were carried through into his axe, shield and helmet.

Below An early design sketch of one of the Orc crutches, which would double as a weapon.

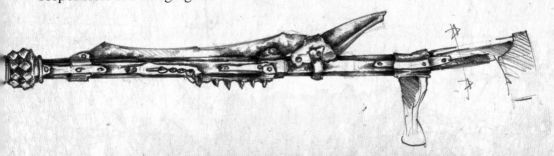

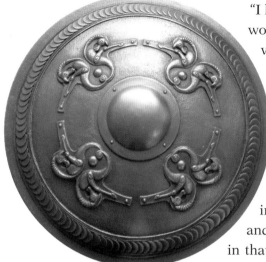

"I knew about Simon and his company when I began working on *The Lord of the Rings*. He came with a very strong recommendation from a friend of mine, and so when this all kicked off I went out to meet him at Shepperton where he was working on a movie. He was very busy, and I'm not sure he realised just why we were there: I think he thought we were just coming round to look at what he was up to. He is an amazing, creative, skilful, patient craftsman and artist, who is incredibly knowledgeable about arms and armour, and the history of warfare, so he's a terrific resource in that respect. However, the level of detail and care in the work is astonishing, I mean genuinely astonishing. We couldn't *not* involve him."

Simon takes up the story himself: "Artisan started off doing work for theatres and a fair amount of museum replica work for body armour. As we went more and more down the route of armour work, with some steel fabrication and quite a lot of moulded-leather work we started to gain a reputation for being detailed and committed. So we started looking for work in TV and film and quite quickly started

Above A Rohan warrior's shield with an equine motif repeated around the central boss.

Right Gimli puts his shield and armour to good use, fending off the Orcs during the battle of Helm's Deep performed by the original Toronto cast.

THE LORD OF THE RINGS

getting more and more work. We did *Troy* and *Alexander, King Arthur, Cold Mountain*. It was while I was running the principal armour department for *Alexander* that I was recommended to Rob Howell by one of the costume coordinators, and he phoned up and arranged a meeting. Irene Bohan, the production's associate costume designer, and Rob came round; they had a look at the workshop, and saw what we were doing. We had a bit of a chat, quite a short meeting, then they went away. About a year later, once *The Lord of the Rings* was officially up and running, Rob re-contacted me and asked if we'd like to join the production.

"One of the most useful things I saw was a run-through with actors back in May 2005. When you first read a script, they always say that you should put it down and not make any notes, just read it and appreciate it. So, having done that, it was really useful getting to see it in a fairly good stage of development because I could bring up questions about the staging such as, 'How's this going to work with twenty guys waving swords?' and 'How's he going to jump up and down like that wearing a big suit of armour?' Those considerations are in there from the first time you pick up a pencil, look at a design, or decide how to make the prop – they're the kind of things that either make you successful or not, if you take them into account. Even when they tell you an actor's going to stand in the background and not move, chances are he'll be in the foreground and leaping off the back of a horse. It's usually what happens, so we always assume that they're going to be quite active in these things. We try to give them as much movement, and to cut down the weight as much as possible, but maintain the structural integrity so it's light as it can be but going to last for a couple of years of hard service.

"So, it was great to watch, to get a feel for how it was going to be staged, and how it sounded, and the look of it – even though a lot of the visual components weren't there. But also on a purely practical level, up until that point I had no real indication of the level of commitment from the production company and whether this was going to be a fantastic, well-funded, serious project or a fantastic, serious, incredibly well-supported project that perhaps didn't have as much money as it should, or a horrible, shambling, tin-pot operation. I really had no idea, so it was good to go and see that, to see a lot of

Overleaf Aragorn commands the Army of the Dead. This scene would be cut for the London production.

Below An early costume design for one of the Army of the Dead. As it would be worn by ensemble actors of varying heights, the use of chain-mail connecting the armour plates allowed it to be flexible enough to comfortably fit them all.

115

people involved in the project in one place and see what they'd done so far; to get a feel for, not so much the level of professionalism, but the level of commitment to the project.

"It's really quite difficult to ascertain where Rob's designs end and mine begin on things like armour. Rob did loads of rough ideas that we tossed back and forth and gradually I steered him in the direction I thought was right to go. It was very collaborative – Rob gave me some fantastic and interesting and challenging designs, some of which were quite focused, and it was just a case of trying to turn them into a functional object or costume. A number of items have come from these fantastically detailed designs, others from some really quite vague sketches, and so those took a lot of time.

"For a lot of the weapon work, Rob pretty much left me to get on with it. I think if he'd had the time he'd have drawn them all up himself, and I would have been very happy for him to have done that, but because he didn't have the time we were quite happy to do it instead. Of course, ultimately it was Rob's show and he got the final say, but some of the more fun times were when he fed me information, then I went back with something and he had already drawn something up since then that actually looked quite similar.

"The whole of our studio works in a similar way. Sometimes I would go to the team with some very specific sketches or a maquette –

A collection of weapon props used by the principal actors, including leaf-shaped blades carried by the hobbits and the mace carried by Boromir.

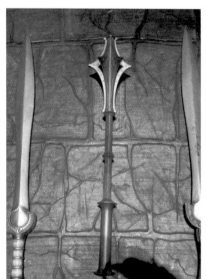
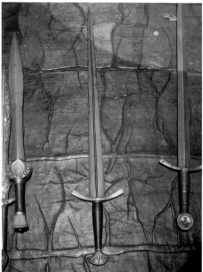
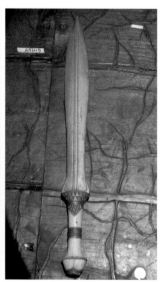

THE LORD OF THE RINGS

a miniature model – or a mock-up and ask someone to turn it into a prototype, and quite often the guys would come to me with a suggestion or push something in a different direction. That kind of feedback is very nice, very rewarding. I wouldn't have it any other way. It was also essential, especially when we were doing the turnaround that we've done for *The Lord of the Rings*: about 200 breastplates, helmets and such like, all capable enough to take the wear and tear of being used night after night for a lengthy theatre run, taking into account that things will be broken or lost. Then there are the weapons, of which we did between 150 and 180 of each. Often with the hero swords and daggers – i.e. the ones used by the main cast rather than the ensemble – we'd make one practical sword, and one medium-quality back-up in case the hero got lost or damaged, which would be very unusual for a production like this.

"It's risky because if a sword like Sting gets broken, you have to use the back-up until a new one can be cast. That said, breakages shouldn't be a problem as our stuff is made to a very high specification but prudence would say that for a job that's going to run eight shows a week for potentially two years, you should have some sort of contingency – and there is, but it's quite tight. Of course, if they find themselves in a position where they do need repeats for a second run of the show in London or New York or wherever, then we'll be set up to do that, because the prototyping's been done and the moulds are ready – the processes for any particular item, whether it's a sword or a piece of armour, will have been honed

Frodo's sword, Sting, an Elven blade given to him by Bilbo. Tolkien wrote that when Orcs were near it would glow blue so Simon Brindle and his team at Artisan created a hollow blade fitted with LED bulbs that could be activated by the actor.

119

down; we know what we're doing, so can turn them around quite quickly.

"It's the same with the costumes. They can be mended or duplicated quite easily, although, again, the hero costumes are terribly accurate and detailed, hand-made every time. Take King Théoden as an example. He wears a scaled tunic base, which is a medium-weight and covered with leather ringlets, two to three millimetres thick – thousands of them individually stitched together. In fact, the costumes belonging to the principals such as Aragorn, Boromir and the others are all made from mostly real materials. They could be moulded leather, cast bronze and brass fittings and a bit of steel fabrication where it's needed.

"For the armies and ensemble, the costumes are a combination of materials. For the Army of the Dead, we're using a real chainmail shirt for the base garment, and then we're using cast rubber and urethane copies for the hard armour or plate armour elements. It's a cost-effective, durable product, and it picks up detail fantastically well. The key to all of these is knowing where to use them, how to use them, and knowing that the material is really only as good as the prototype or the original. For example, let's say we're making a piece of steel plate armour for the upper body: it has moving parts and articulated layers, it needs to fit very well and function well and move smoothly. Whether you reproduce that in plastic or hardened leather or steel, it still needs to do all that, and if, despite the work being put in at the start, it doesn't function correctly, it won't matter what the material is, it's still not going to be a comfortable thing to wear.

"The Dead armour was quite interesting, actually, just in terms of its constructional complexity. For the ensemble armours or, if you like, the army pieces, whether it's film or theatre or TV, you're always asked to provide a one-size-fits-all garment, which happens with varying degrees of success! I'd like to think, as far as Artisan is concerned, that it's usually quite successful. Sometimes, such as on this production, it could be quite tricky given they've cast five-foot-six and below, quite lithe and slim circus performers for the hobbits and dwarves, then over six-foot-two for the Rohan soldiers and the Army of the Dead! These are ensemble guys, so you have to have a piece of armour that's going to go from a 38-inch, five-foot-six guy up to a 44-

inch, six-foot-two guy. The constructional complexities of putting together a piece of armour that's going to function and still be comfortable on both was quite a challenge and the Army of the Dead in that respect was a little bit out of the ordinary. I think we've managed to solve it quite well by using expanding chain-mail panels, and a combination of the chain-mail itself and the lower-body pieces.

"In addition to the armour, there were the Orc masks to consider. The helmet part is cast urethane, but the facemasks are actually moulded leather, which is very effective because it keeps its shape incredibly well while still giving some flexibility. It's a natural material so there's some permeability – the material breathes a little bit – making it very comfortable to wear. Using these materials also means that when we repeat-mould the face masks we can get an almost infinite number of variations out of just three or four different face moulds, merely by laying the leather in with different creases and twists and stitching it together

The Orc captains were given raised metal crowns on their helmets, both to signify their elevated status among Saruman's army and to draw attention to these particular performers from the original Toronto cast, who on occasion will play a great part in events on the stage.

THE OFFICIAL STAGE COMPANION

Right A prosthetic mask of one of the Orcs; with the teeth of the mouth-brace painted a garish decaying yellow the Orc-face takes on a terrifying look.

Below A sculpture of a potential Orc-head, to see how the helmet will look.

in different ways. We can achieve what Rob wanted from the start, which is a variety of different Orcs in a reasonably cost-effective way, just through a good choice of materials.

"Similarly, the material used to construct the weapons is also urethane, but of a slightly different type – it's still a dense urethane polymer, but essentially it's pretty much rubber. It's quite hefty, though, because it's injection-moulded under pressure around a fibreglass armature, and its density means that it has quite a long usable life. Some of the weapons will have a steel or aluminium armature running through and because the mix is an expanding foam, it has to be injected. The result is that when you pick one up you might think there's a reasonable amount of weight to it but actually compared to a steel equivalent it's considerably lighter.

"Just a handful of the principal weapons feature hand-forged steel blades – originally, there was a possibility the whole production would go with steel, but that would have been a financial stretch. Also, there is a safety issue with steel weapons. Basically, there's a vast array of materials you can use to make weaponry. Among the best are combat-quality, high-carbon steel blades, and foam urethane, or cast-rubber, blades. Those are probably your best choices: functional weapons which can be used repeatedly and which can take a good hammering. The benefits of steel blades are that ultimately they are much more hard-wearing, sound great, look great and you can do a lot with balancing the pommel to alleviate the extra weight of the blade. But the safety issue is that even though it's a precision-milled piece of hard-carbon steel, it's chosen for its subtleness so there's flex in the blade but it's not so soft that it's going to chew at the edges. This means there's always a risk you'll get a stress fracture and the top six or twelve inches will go spinning off into the audience!

"A sword can last you twenty years, but you never really know if that's going to happen. There's always that potential safety risk. It can be reduced by careful maintenance and redrafting of the blade, but it's something you have to do after every show. The benefits of rubber are many: there is not that safety issue, full stop, plus you can get fantastic relief detail into the blades, as well as the pommel and grip. It's much easier to create – you can really go to town on the blades, with beautifully creative surface relief, detail and engravings, and you can repeat the pattern again and again in rubber and it'll look fantastic every time. The drawback is that it's rubber: it's not as hard and ultimately as durable, and so it has a limited usable life.

The Orc crutches are stored safely away in order to minimize the risk of damage between performances.

THE OFFICIAL STAGE COMPANION

Gimli (Ross Williams) and Aragorn (Evan Builing). Every detail of the actors' costumes was designed to look and feel authentic, right down to Aragorn's travelling bag.

But it does mean that Actor A can't accidentally run Actor B through with it, which is, one imagines, a huge benefit. It's still going to hurt, though, if you get smacked round the head with one!"

Rob Tannion mentioned earlier that he was looking forward to training his performers to use the Orc crutches: part-support device, part-bladed weapon, wholly unpleasant. How did they come about?

"The Orc crutches originate entirely from Rob Howell's concept for these 'experiments gone wrong', which is how he described his whole concept for the Orcs. Their hunched, body suits with built-up shoulders and grotesque, stretched faces with added steel mouth braces completely come from Rob. He wanted the contrast between these experimented-upon creatures, which make you almost feel sorry for because they're hobbling around on crutches, but yet, irrespective of how malformed they are, they're basically evil creatures. We've turned their supports into something nasty to chop off your arms and for other foul deeds. It's an interesting attempt to marry the vulnerability of these creatures with their murderous and evil intent.

"Rob's remit for this entire production was to try to keep the arms and armoury reasonably authentic. Obviously, Middle-earth is an invented world and there's just such a vast array of material already there. The original text is actually very specific in areas and so, to some degree, that's helped. For the kingdom of Rohan, there's a mid to late Romano-British, slightly Celtic influence going on. This is quite apparent in the original text, and has obviously been picked

WE'VE TURNED THEIR SUPPORTS INTO SOMETHING NASTY TO CHOP OFF YOUR ARMS AND FOR OTHER FOUL DEEDS. IT'S AN INTERESTING ATTEMPT TO MARRY THE VULNERABILITY OF THESE CREATURES WITH THEIR MURDEROUS AND EVIL INTENT.

up in the films, so a lot of time was spent looking at the original reference material, working from Rob's direction and input, and then checking that against primary reference and research, which is always a good thing to do.

"Unlike Rob I'd seen the films – in fact I'd seen the first one before I knew anything about this show – so I couldn't avoid it. I was aware of the fact that I could spend a long time sketching something up and push it in a certain direction, and come back to it a couple of days later to realise that I'd totally and subconsciously reproduced something I'd seen three years before at an art exhibition or in one of the films. In that respect, I think everyone finds themselves recreating something, or a feel of something, that they've seen elsewhere and liked or appreciated. Because I'm aware of that, I didn't avoid looking at other references; in fact, I brought in books on the films because we didn't want to reproduce what they did. I wanted to make sure that the designs that Rob gave me, and the pieces that we generated ourselves, are entirely unique to the show.

"One of Rob's main design themes was the overall silhouette of an object. The line of it and the shape was critical, whether it's plain or massively detailed, and was something to which we paid a huge amount of attention. So for anything we created we got the silhouette and shape right before we worried about the detail. There's the old maxim that form should follow function. The detail is then sympathetic to the silhouette; but for a stage show the level of detail and

Three early conceptual designs for the Orcs; the two on the left have the fan-like crests of captains, whereas the righthand Orc is merely a foot-soldier. At this stage, the crutches had much more pronounced blades.

THE OFFICIAL STAGE COMPANION

Opposite Gollum (Michael Therriault) shows off his full-body make-up and sparse but effective costume. The enlarged knees and elbows enhance the emaciated look of the creature while also providing protection as he cavorts around the stage. Make-up is used to shade his ribs and allow the stomach to appear sunken, and he wears prosthetic extensions on his fingers to lengthen the arms.

finish on our armour and weaponry is much greater than it needed to be. Why? Firstly, because it's something that Rob requested and it's one of the reasons why he came to me. The other reason is that we were all well aware of the fact that if this show is successful there are going to be twenty-foot posters up outside the theatres; there are going to be magazine covers; and there may even be books written about our work, as there was about the weaponry in the films. It's not that we're vain and want to represent ourselves fantastically well and waste money; rather it's that we want to do the best possible job. We've really put our hearts into this show and given them much more than they asked for – because we wanted to do the stuff that Rob wanted to see, and we enjoyed making the props to such a high standard. If you take a piece of armour or a weapon three-quarters of the way to where it needs to be, you may as well do that last quarter anyway, just for personal satisfaction. We haven't unnecessarily applied details just for the sake of it – I think it would be quite apparent if we had because, although you might not notice from thirty feet, you probably will from fifteen and you definitely will from five – and if it's not been done in the right way, it'll just look like over-decorated cake, and no one wants that!"

Detail is terribly important in aspects of design. Charged with overseeing the creation of the costumes was Irene Bohan, who explains how she and Rob Howell delineated the project.

"Rob and I worked together on the initial research – we kicked ideas around between us, Rob did some drawings, then I followed those up with working drawings for the costume cutters; we then went through the finished results together – it was very collaborative. It was also my job to coordinate getting everything physically made, sorting out the fabrics, sourcing materials. This took me all over the world as I looked for different styles and textures. We even went to Helsinki to look at Finnish folk costumes as inspiration for the hobbits – because Tolkien himself had been interested in the Finnish language, so it seemed a good place to start for his major characters. I don't think any of it is reflected directly in the final costumes, but there's lots of little things, motifs and materials, that were inspired by them.

"Gollum was the most interesting challenge. Rob had pretty clear ideas about the surface texture of Gollum's skin but we didn't

THE LORD OF THE RINGS

WE INITIALLY LOOKED AT BODY SUITS, BUT NONE OF US REALLY WANTED TO GO DOWN THAT ROUTE, BECAUSE NO MATTER HOW MUCH YOU DRESS IT UP, IT STILL LOOKS LIKE A PIECE OF DANCEWEAR.

Previous **A montage of early costume designs showing the wide variety of colour, shape, texture and pattern of the various characters, so that each character will look distinctive, regardless of how little time they spend on the stage.**

get going on the designs until we started rehearsals in Canada – he was therefore the last thing that we did. We thought the design work needed to be done in conjunction with Michael Therriault, the actor playing Gollum, who was terribly interested and full of good ideas. After all, there was no point in us saying to him 'This is what you are going to wear', him taking the character and movement in a completely different direction and so we end up with something impractical or restrictive. We initially looked at body suits, but none of us really wanted to go down that route, because no matter how much you dress it up, it still looks like a piece of dancewear. Then Michael began bringing in photos and other references for bodyshapes that he would incorporate into his performance, so we ended up with an idea of Rob's, where Gollum's body, his skin, looked almost as though it was stitched together. It was a real case of where do the rags start and the flesh end?

A collection of wigs await their Lothlórien Elf wearers.

"We were lucky enough to find a guy in Canada who's invented a new kind of prosthetic that is self-sticking. So the make-up artists worked with us a lot, and we were able to create these prosthetics with a stitched fabric base and apply them directly on to Michael's body. We'd soak the body pieces in this formula and they would adhere directly to the skin; and there was no having to take it off after the show with chemicals. It's a slow process, involving lots of people, but terribly worthwhile, because obviously you don't want Michael to have to undergo having his entire body covered in spirit gum eight times a week. It was always going to be important to involve the actor, because for a role like Gollum we knew no one was just going to turn up on the first day and know how it was going to be played from the off. We had to learn as a team the way the character would move and react and create a workable, practical costume design round that. We had to be as flexible as him. Michael was very enthusiastic and full of ideas.

"The choice to go with wholly organic fabrics narrowed the field of materials but it wasn't a burden. Certainly, it was harder to find natural fabrics than it used to be but that's the challenge – we wanted to ensure that there wasn't anything in the show that hadn't first been distressed, dyed or treated. The result was that nothing looked brand new; it was all made to look worn and lived in.

Above A huge number of costumes have to be kept in precisely ordered ranks, so that the wardrobe crew can ensure the ensemble actors make their costume changes without mishap or delay.

"For instance, the original Galadriel gown needed to be something that had real resonance with her environment, and we knew it had to be a lightweight fabric; so I scoured materials from all over the world and eventually found just what I wanted. Then, of course, it got dyed, foil-printed and changed beyond all recognition! It's a lengthy process, not remotely straightforward, and one I knew would stretch me – that was the appeal. And although it was a lengthy process, Rob and I were determined that there was nothing in the show that you could go out and buy in shops – everything was made from scratch. In a show like this, there are usually some things, even if they're just shoes, that you can buy off the rack – but not in *The Lord of the Rings*. Everything had to be made from scratch – it was a challenge but a remarkably refreshing one, and one that made us all that little bit more creative, It really drew on my knowledge of cloth as well as dance and movement, knowing what would and wouldn't be practical in the final show.

"We were able to sit down with Peter Darling and discuss his choreography to ensure that the costumes we were constructing looked right for us but also had the freedom of movement that Peter needed for his performers. The armour was always the most difficult in terms of movement but Simon from Artisan came over to do the fittings so any adjustments could be made easily. Plus, in Canada, we had a very experienced team who knew armour as well, and so they could adapt as we went along."

The CHOREOGRAPHY

aving looked at the way the costumes, armour and weaponry is constructed, let's return to Peter Darling and Rob Tannion and ask how Simon's work co-exists alongside their choreography. Surely it must be daunting trying to find performers who can do the dancing, singing and acting required to be Orcs or Ents while working with these props?

"It's a collaborative thing," Peter confirms. "The audition process can be very much like a tug of war, where Matthew is concentrating on actors and Christopher Nightingale is focusing on good singers. So it's a case of, 'I want this person… you give me them and you can have that one,' because you know that you need certain people for certain things, but at the same time they need to be able to sing like demons!

"Another factor is that we started off in Canada where the talent pool is quite different from, say, the UK. In the UK we have a history of multitasking performers, whereas elsewhere they have different strengths, different requirements, perhaps because a lot of the shows that they have in Toronto are those big shows that have been done before, so the requirements are very clear. They're perhaps more jazz-based and so the people we have found are potentially very exciting, even though some of them have perhaps not, in terms of movement, had the kind of experience that I'm interested in. So we're not just choreographing; in some cases, we're teaching new skills from scratch."

Rob is equally excited at this prospect: "Peter and I have been discussing the sort of things we can start implementing into a daily class or prior to the rehearsals, because we've got a range of people, from those who come from a strong movement background to actors

Opposite Each of the Orc performers of the original Toronto production was choreographed with a particular set of movements for the time when they are on stage.

133

THE OFFICIAL STAGE COMPANION

primarily trained with few movement skills. Finding something that's going to be useful for everyone is again a task on its own, and to train everyone up, getting them to start thinking in a different way about the sort of movement that we're going to ask them to do is good fun. It's not going to be given to them on a plate so much as us noting that a couple of them have potential to be sent off on their own to see if they can work some ideas out, then come back to Peter and I to hone them, giving them the skills to take it further.

"Often, some of the more interesting movements can be created when it comes from, say, thirty different minds rather than just our two. When we did the auditions, we put the performers through their paces. We got them to do a slow, elegiac piece, and then we'd do an obstacle course, and it was very revealing because often the two didn't come together.

"And this is when the juggling act starts, as I'm wanting to teach them to move like Orcs, Matthew wants them to learn lines as Breelanders, Christopher wants to make them sing for the *Prancing Pony* sequences and Alex wants to put them on giant stilts and be

In addition to each set of ensemble performers being trained to move and fight in a different way, depending on which army they belong to, lighting is used to partition sections of the stage to create scenes within scenes, as seen here during the original Toronto production.

WHEN WE DID THE AUDITIONS, WE PUT THE PERFORMERS THROUGH THEIR PACES. WE GOT THEM TO DO A SLOW, ELEGIAC PIECE, AND THEN WE'D DO AN OBSTACLE COURSE, AND IT WAS VERY REVEALING BECAUSE OFTEN THE TWO DIDN'T COME TOGETHER.

Ents. So it's a juggling act to get enough time with everyone, but as long as you are always thinking that the most important thing is the show, as opposed to 'Oh, my sequences are being sacrificed', then you're likely to succeed in terms of getting good final results. For instance, because we only have the stage floor for three weeks of the rehearsal period, Christopher, who would normally do his music in that first week, is holding back in order that we can really work the company on the floor – and obviously I will have to return the favour. I think these things do arise, but if there's enough communication then you can relax. For instance, on one occasion I was talking to Matthew about where he wanted all the Elves to come on in Lothlórien: 'From one entrance?' And he replied, 'Well, no, actually it's up to you. I don't mind.' This saved a lot of time, as I wasn't going to be setting up one set of movements only to find out later it didn't suit his ideas."

The man responsible for bringing the circus skills to the table is Alex Frith, of AirCraft Performance.

"I was teaching an acrobatics class," Alex explains of his introduction to *The Lord of the Rings*. "Matthew, Kevin and Rob Howell had all come down, and they were looking at a woman named Kirsten Little working on some specially made tall stilts. I was just teaching, working with a group, putting them through a whole set of drills and making them do lots of exercises, and they liked the way I dealt with my group and trained my class. They were looking for someone to be a physical trainer on the show, and also to teach stilts and be a circus consultant. I had done a Dance degree in Australia, then came over to the UK and got involved in the Millennium Dome big show, and that's where the whole circus thing got into my blood.

"I saw *The Lord of the Rings* as a series of challenges. It wasn't my job to see the big picture, rather to come up with solutions for the problems they had envisioning the movements for things such as the Black Riders, Shelob and the Ents. How to make those three things work? So I collaborated with Rob Howell and looked at his designs, had a number of meetings with him, and then went off to my workshop and developed what was needed. It's been a couple of years' work for me, getting these ideas up and running, which has been great.

"Then, as time went on, Peter Darling and Rob Tannion got involved, and we've tended to solve these things together, going to Delstar for a couple of weeks and working out what could and could not be done on the stage, utilising the lifts and revolve to best effect. It's evolved from me being an outside circus consultant, to really becoming a part of the creative team, which I'm really pleased about that. Working with Rob Tannion has been fantastic. He's got an incredible grounding in physical theatre, and seeing the way he approaches a task has influenced me a lot. It's been about just playing with different options and seeing what happens, then work from there. It's about fully exploring things as well; not allowing myself to become rushed or hurried and putting enough time into exhausting all the possibilities with one element.

One of the most complex scenes to choreograph was the song at *The Prancing Pony* inn at Bree. The four hobbit leads, together with a multitude of other cast from the original Toronto production, perform a head-spinning array of energetic dance moves. Benches that were originally held up to represent wall-slats of the three-storied inn (note the windows painted on the lower benches in the middle picture) are now used as dance aids and even springboards.

"I think that's what Peter does a lot. You're saying, 'Oh, it's not working,' and he'll reply, 'Just stay with it. It's interesting; there's something there...' He's very good at spotting the things that might work, then bringing in a video of, say, Chinese opera and pointing out the way they move their heads, and telling Rob and I, 'I don't know what it is, but see what you can do with that.' Then we go off and work on that and Peter will come in and say, 'Play with these astrojax and see what you can do with them, and balance this candle on your head and dance around and see what comes from that.' From all this we develop material, which begins to create a picture; all these different things building up a bigger picture. Peter's living the creation of the work all the time – he's got his video camera with him all the time and even if he sees something on the television, he videos it off the TV; often it just looks like a few blurs but if you look you can see what he's seeing there. On one occasion he had captured these twins on *Oprah*, who were just these little old men, but what they were doing with their heads was just pure hobbitry. Another time he had us watching *Watership Down* and looking at the rabbits and the way rabbits move; looking at their physicality. Peter's approach was fascinating, and informed much of what we were doing with physical performance on this show."

THE OFFICIAL STAGE COMPANION

ONE THING ALEX HAS BEEN VERY HEAVILY INVOLVED WITH, POSSIBLY MORE THAN ANYONE ELSE, HAS BEEN THE MOVEMENT AND IMAGE OF THE BLACK RIDERS.

Opposite It is easy to forget that the terrifying Black Rider (Nicholas Gede-Lange) creature and his steed are just one man.

Below The horse head of this first prototype is attached to Alex Frith's legs as well as to his wrists; this keeps the head a constant distance from him while also helping to support the frame. Two rods allow him to move the head in well-rehearsed and realistic sweeps.

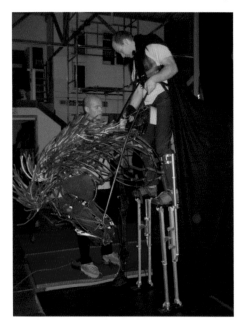

One thing Alex has been very heavily involved with, possibly more than anyone else, has been the movement and image of the Black Riders.

"To begin with, Rob had a model – he had literally got a plastic horse, cut off its legs, stuck a man in it, draped a cloth over them and so created an illusion of a black horse from one side, with a cape, a head and a rider. He then spun it around and I saw that there were just two stilts holding it up. They had done some stilt tests already but asked me what sort of stilts they could use to do the Riders. I said they could use either pegs or Duras. With pegs, you've got to keep treading on, keep moving to maintain your balance, but with Duras you can stand still, rather like dry-wall-plaster stilts.

"I made the decision very early on that, for a big costume like this – for the weight and the strength that it would need – it had to be 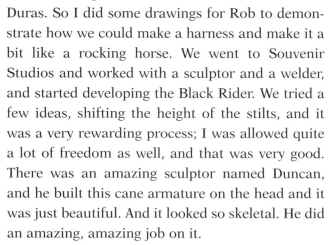 Duras. So I did some drawings for Rob to demonstrate how we could make a harness and make it a bit like a rocking horse. We went to Souvenir Studios and worked with a sculptor and a welder, and started developing the Black Rider. We tried a few ideas, shifting the height of the stilts, and it was a very rewarding process; I was allowed quite a lot of freedom as well, and that was very good. There was an amazing sculptor named Duncan, and he built this cane armature on the head and it was just beautiful. And it looked so skeletal. He did an amazing, amazing job on it.

"Then there were the Ents to sort out. They are on three-metre stilts – so really quite tall – and I had to train twenty people to learn how to walk on them, people who had never done stilt-walking

138

THE LORD OF THE RINGS

before. In London, it's fairly easy to find stilt-walkers who can act and sing but we weren't sure how easy it was going to be in Toronto. Of course, there's a huge circus tradition in Canada because of the French influence – Montreal, in fact, has got a fantastic circus ethic, but while you could get the most amazing performer there, they only speak French, they absolutely sound French and don't speak English. So, unless the Ents are suddenly all going to come from Paris, you're stuck.

"But we overcame all these problems eventually – Peter worked hard on finding the right people who could multi-task, and the idea of the Ents as tall people rather than tree-creatures was a brilliant solution. If the actors had been stuck in big rubber suits, looking like trees with wood all over them, it would have been really disappointing for the audience. The performers had to do three weeks' intensive training, full-time, all day every day. I started them on half a metre, then a metre, and built it up. They're also all on a retractable safety wire, like a car seatbelt, for the

A rank of stilts which will support the Ent performers. Only the bottoms of the stilts have been painted as the rest of the pole will be hidden by the Ents' long coats.

show as well. Even if they're very competent, the best in the world even, we can't take any risks; and if one was to go down, they all would go down – the domino effect. It's not going to look cool, but more importantly, you could die from three metres if you fall in the wrong way. So these wires stop the performer and can control them coming down if we need to, or keep them in one space, which is great. They've also all got poles, a staff, so they can balance on three points, which is going to make a big difference to their confidence."

Writer Shaun McKenna remains very excited by the work being done on bringing the Ents to life. "I was delighted with the stilts idea for the

THE LORD OF THE RINGS

Ents because they were some of my favourite characters when I read the book. I loved Treebeard, and was really sorry that we couldn't put him in – originally I think he had one line when he grabbed Merry and Pippin but that was it. So the notion of being able to find a theatrical way to give the Ents a physical presence, so they weren't just going to be men in tree suits, was really good and very exciting."

One has to wonder at the enormity of what is being placed upon these multitasking performers. Not only will they be singing, acting, fighting and dancing, but often with unwieldy props or heavy costumes with half-masks restricting their vision; and there will be many quick changes – an actor may begin as a Breelander, then be required to be a Gondorian and even an Orc as well. It must surely represent a nightmare not just for the actors, but also the choreographers.

"I'm a firm believer that what you don't want to do is set your bar at the lowest level," responds Peter with a smile to this particular set of problems. "You want to set the bar really high, and then just chip away downwards until you get to something that is workable and practical. That is something that we discovered as we went along, that there were certain things that we just needed to get rid of because the costume didn't allow for it."

"Also, we had to think a lot about safety," Rob adds. "Obviously, something that'll be great in terms of look, or a costume, has to be practical and safe. Our primary focus is the well-being of the per-formers and making sure that they're going to be able to do eight shows a week on a consistent, repetitive basis. What we don't want is to end up having injuries. There would be no point in having rehearsed, opened the show and then have half the company off. So we were always trying things out. We'd already spent quite a while looking at different costumes, trying them out, trying out the shoes: 'Okay, if the shoes were a bit more like this…' 'No, actually someone's going to trip over instantly if we have them like that…' 'But they look really good.' 'Yes, but they're impractical, there's no line of sight.' The Orc-masks were significantly altered because of this last point. Looking good is important, but if no one can see more than three inches ahead, it's potentially lethal."

The SPIDER

Moving on from half-blind Orcs, we come to Shelob, the giant spider-like creature that stands between the hobbits and Mordor.

"Shelob was fun to be involved with," says Peter. "I think with her there was something unique and interesting to be done with the puppeteers, exploring how Shelob moves."

"The important thing to remember is that there are many different elements in this show," says Rob Tannion; "there's fight choreography, circus skills, there's a lot of puppetry – all of these things tend to come under the movement area of the show and, essentially, Peter did need to have an overall view of how they work. We wanted Shelob to have a more languid quality so she could attack in a way that surprises the audience. Things like that really did need Peter's overall view and focus."

Alex Frith agrees, observing that he had quite a bit to do with the evolution of the spider. "We had lots of different ideas for Shelob. She was the one thing I did the most work on, really trying to come up with an idea. Then we met Brian Herring, a puppet maker, and we began talking… Rob Howell and I had discussed previously about suspending her from a cherry-picker but we decided that would have been just too big, too mechanical, and we didn't want to do that.

"Brian showed us a video of some work he'd done. I then went and worked with one of his associates and put together a very simple design using carbon-fibre rods and arms that could be operated by the puppeteer, and made quite a dynamic creature. The spider design was then handed over to the Paragon Design team in Ontario, led by Grace Nakatsu, who did a lot of the work on the

Left Toronto rehearsals
with a skeletal form
of the spider, Shelob,
before the full prop is
put in place.

stage version of *The Lion King*, and they made the telescopic boom arm and every other part of the mechanism in Canada. Meanwhile, I continued to be involved with the movement, sorting out how Shelob's attendants, these little old ladies, would move and actually carry her."

Again we find this crossover between movement and design, this time involving Rob Howell's concepts of the giant spider. Of all the things that he prepared for *The Lord of the Rings*, Rob says that Shelob was the one that caused the most… if not headaches, then certainly a few late nights.

"We did so many research and development workshops, because it would be too late, come November and December, just before the show opens, to find out that the ideas we had eighteen months previously were simply not very good ones, or that the spider didn't actually work technically. Ultimately, it took us the longest time to

Overleaf Sam (Peter Howe) defends a mortally wounded Frodo (James Loye) from the monstrous spider during this scene from the original Toronto production. The figures surrounding Shelob are her acolytes, who guide the spider using rods connected to her legs.

THE OFFICIAL STAGE COMPANION

When seen from a hobbit's perspective, the giant spider makes for a terrifying sight. The mechanical arm which supports the spider's body, together with the poles attached to her legs, can be seen here.

arrive at something that didn't feel as if we had given her over completely to acrobatics and circus skills.

"The danger, once we decided that we wanted to include extraordinary physical skills in the production, is that if you're not careful, you get carried away by the excellence of the performers and the story actually stops, which for a fast-paced event is not desirable. There were some extraordinary movement things we were tempted by, and an enormous spider is obviously an area where that losing focus could have happened.

"One other thing we were terribly conscious of was that Shelob is the only female dark force in the story and that we should somehow acknowledge that. That's quite a complicated thing to do with something so big, without making it look like you've been distracted by the femininity and you haven't dealt with the spider. So we knew she needed to be enormous and have this female texture, this ingredient, a feminine spirit. Eight legs, of course, meant that if we were going to manipulate the legs in any way there needed to be eight puppeteers, so we opted to export the femininity of the spider to the puppeteers and let them carry that feminine spirit. Then the spider is free to be something a little more abstract and her silhouette and textures aren't going to be confused or encumbered by the need to carry this feminine quality.

"I think we have achieved a good balance. We have the Ents appearing as men on stilts and we have these women puppeteers with the terrifying spider shape. And the scale and agility of it is such that we can do all the things that you'd want to do with something of Shelob's size and let the audience be genuinely frightened both by her and her attendants, who are these toothless European funereal hags. Again, they're a familiar stereotype: these black-clad Mediterranean women, wearing slightly scary clogs, gathered skirts and headscarves. The fact that they're European seems to be another reference to Tolkien, and yet they're completely out of period, in terms of the Medieval world that the rest of Mordor is represented by. But that's good. We're not trying to tell the audience to take an interest in who these people are specifically – they're not in the story, what they're there for is just to support this feminine silhouette for us."

AFTERWORD

The SHOW GOES EVER ON

Every time a book is adapted for another medium, whether for a film, a TV series or a stage production, the story evolves. That evolution continues with every remake and every new version, and nowhere is this more apparent than in the world of live theatre. After the success of the production in Toronto, playing to more than 420,000 people over a period of seven months, it was perhaps inevitable that it would undergo some changes before reopening in London the following year. With every element of *The Lord of the Rings* having already pushed theatrical boundaries to create a complex and thrilling show the Canadian cast and crew could be proud of, the move to London wasn't going to be just a straightforward case of picking up the show and dropping it on to a London stage. There would be new challenges, from installing the state-of-the-art hydraulic stage in the Theatre Royal, Drury Lane, with its National Heritage protection as a listed building – a very different proposition from the ultra-modern Princess of Wales Theatre in Toronto – to taking account of audience feedback about how Tolkien's story played out on stage. Even recasting the show would inject different ideas, as always happens when introducing a new company of actors to a performance. That concept of organic development which had been the watchword of this entire production over the last few years was still very much in evidence.

One of the seventeen hydraulic lifts of the stage is tested.

"In the original previews in February 2006," explains Matthew Warchus, "the show ran at about three hours and forty minutes. That felt too long, so by April we were down to a manageable three hours twenty – mainly by slimming a few scenes down and cutting out a whole sequence featuring the Paths of the Dead. By the time we were bringing it to London a year later, I felt confident that we could lose a further twenty minutes, to hit three hours. We assessed it all – trim thirty seconds from the flight to the ford, lose a minute from the Bree dance, and we made a very radical choice to cut the prologue entirely. We have condensed and moved part of Act 2 into Act 3, specifically 'Galadriel's Song', which has tightened up the whole Lothlórien sequence – by becoming shorter, it has become more dynamic and provides the extra energy needed to propel the story forward. It's all quite subtle – audiences probably would not even notice unless we pointed out the changes to them – but hopefully more rewarding."

Moving a show into a new theatre is a major operation, especially when the theatre is as grand as the Theatre Royal, Drury Lane. Many rows of seats have been removed while the stage is installed and the sound and lighting re-programmed for the new venue. Eventually the seats will be replaced, wrapping the audience around the circular stage.

The steel framework of the circular stage, whose foundations descend deep into the lower levels of the Theatre Royal, Drury Lane.

The change to the Lothlórien musical sequence which opens Act 2 also impacted upon designer Rob Howell. "The Elven gowns were originally ceremonial, regal, appropriate to a place of serenity, of calm and rest. But now the look of the Elves has been adjusted to reflect a new, brasher mood. If you make a set, costumes, performance and music too soothing and relaxed, your audience gets too relaxed as well and there's a danger they might lose concentration."

Christopher Nightingale should be delighted that, along with Michael Therriault as Gollum, James Loye as Frodo and Peter Howe as Sam are transferring from the Toronto production to London. "We came to realize that Frodo and Sam provide the crucial emotional connection with the audience. If we weren't careful, we could try to be so true to all the detail in the book that the non-Tolkien fans in the audience could spend too long trying to figure out the story and not enough time caring about the characters. In the end, this is a simple story of two hobbits, their friendship and their mission."

Writer Shaun McKenna sympathises with this feeling that too close an adherence to Tolkien's original story could curtail the experience that live theatre offers. "There are some amazing set

THE LORD OF THE RINGS

pieces, such as the battle of Helm's Deep, an essential aspect of the story. It was a fantastic technical achievement, but the early Canadian audiences had already been blown away by so many events and spectacles that Helm's Deep maybe felt like just another in a line. So after the first ten days of previews we began to make all three acts leaner, meaner and tighter and ensured that the emotional story shone through at the points it really needed to."

Shaun McKenna certainly wasn't daunted by the challenges the move to London threw his way. "We needed to let go our complete fidelity to the original book. The reaction from the Tolkien fans in Toronto was so supportive, which was gratifying. Despite our earlier fears, no one said they missed Faramir or other secondary characters, indeed they appreciated the subtle references written especially for them, so we've felt able to trim back a tiny bit more without actually throwing anything away."

The biggest change for everyone in the UK production has been

Below Gandalf (Brent Carver) is imprisoned by Saruman in his tower of Orthanc, the single spotlight making for an effective cell.

the physical change of venue. "In Toronto, we were in a theatre that was sympathetic to the look of our show, so that it never detracted," Rob Howell says. "Drury Lane is a Grade 1 listed building, so we cannot say things like 'if we took that wall away, our sets would fit better'. In Toronto we were able to take away almost all of their concrete stage, revealing a big basement we could fill with our lifts, and so bring the staging further forward – as a result, they've been left with a theatre that's far more adaptable now to other shows. We've all been very sensitive about not damaging the Drury Lane theatre, although National Heritage have been enormously co-operative in accepting that it's a working building and there needs to be a compromise from all theatres that want to have shows playing in them. We found a balance where the building is

THE OFFICIAL STAGE COMPANION

Both sides prepare for the final battle for Middle-earth; although the storm clouds have gathered sunlight is beginning to shine through in this climactic scene from the original Toronto production.

unaffected but we can retain the immediacy, the contact with the audience. For example, we've built a false proscenium in front of the stage to add to the illusion of the world breaking out into the audience. I want the audience to be unaware of technology – no flashing lights, no visible speakers, so everyone can buy into the idea this is a whole world removed from our reality.

If anything at all has dampened the creative team's excitement about opening in London's West End, it is perhaps the disappointment that the Toronto run couldn't have carried on even longer. Shaun McKenna is clear on this. "We never set out for Toronto to be a 'try out', but historically others are bound to see it as that. Toronto was a damn good show, it was 95% perfect, and it would have got even better had it continued. That continuation now has to be in London."

Matthew Warchus agrees. "Maybe a different 5% will change when it goes to other countries, whether Germany, Japan, Australia or the USA. Nothing can be 100% successful; the more artistic you are, the less able you are to achieve everything in your vision. For me, the excitement of theatre is that every night is different. But if it works as a production, if the audiences enjoy it, then I will be extremely proud, because I know more than anyone else what it has entailed to get to this point."

The Lord of the Rings has been a long journey. As Rob Howell explains, it's had an interesting if unexpected parallel: "Kevin kept saying that we were in our own real-life Fellowship of the Ring situation. Our journey in putting this show together has been like Frodo's, in that we didn't know where we were going at the beginning but knew roughly where we needed to get to, and there was a group of us all committed to travelling that road together. Yet whereas the Fellowship were on their way to destroy something small, we have been trying to create something huge!"

But for the last word, let's go back to the man behind the whole event, Kevin Wallace.

"I believe in the power of theatre to tell huge, epic, and at the same time touching, intimate stories, as it has since ancient times. As an ex-actor myself, it thrills me that no matter how much money or how much scale is involved, in the end it comes down to the script and the honesty of the performance. I am proud that the people we brought together, combining expertise in words, music and drama, have proved absolutely to be the right team to retell J.R.R. Tolkien's primal story of Frodo and Sam's journey to live audiences. *The Lord of the Rings* actually makes quintessentially great theatre, something many people argued couldn't be done, and to have achieved it is a legacy I hope we can all be proud of."

Gollum (Michael Therriault) stands on the brink of triumph and disaster at the Crack of Doom, watched by the Eye of Sauron.

CREDITS: TORONTO

KEVIN WALLACE and SAUL ZAENTZ
in association with DAVID & ED MIRVISH, and MICHAEL COHL

Book and Lyrics by SHAUN McKENNA
and MATTHEW WARCHUS

Music by
A.R. RAHMAN
VÄRTTINÄ
with CHRISTOPHER NIGHTINGALE

Set and Costume Designer ROB HOWELL

Lighting Designer PAUL PYANT
Sound Designer SIMON BAKER (for Autograph)
Musical Supervisor CHRISTOPHER NIGHTINGALE
Moving Image Direction by THE GRAY CIRCLE
Literary Consultant LAURIE BATTLE
Special Effects Designer GREGORY MEEH
Illusions and Magic Effects PAUL KIEVE
Musical Director RICK FOX

Associate Choreographer ROB TANNION Circus Skills Specialist ALEX FRITH Fight Director TERRY KING
Associate Costume Designer IRENE BOHAN Associate Set Designer MEGAN HUISH Associate Lighting Designer DAVID HOWE
Associate Sound Designer STEN SEVERSON Production Stage Manager THE. JOHN GRAY Associate Musical Supervisor RICHARD BROWN
Casting STEPHANIE GORIN (Canada), MAGGIE LUNN (UK) Resident Director ALISA PALMER

Orchestrations by CHRISTOPHER NIGHTINGALE, A.R. RAHMAN and VÄRTTINÄ

Choreographer PETER DARLING

Directed by MATTHEW WARCHUS

THE CAST

In order of speaking

Frodo Baggins, a hobbit .... JAMES LOYE	Elrond Halfelven, Lord of Rivendell .... VICTOR A. YOUNG
Sam Gamgee, a hobbit, Frodo's gardener .... PETER HOWE	Arwen Evenstar, Elrond's daughter .... CARLY STREET
Rosie Cotton, a hobbit .... KRISTIN GALER	Bilbo Baggins, a hobbit, Frodo's uncle .... CLIFF SAUNDERS
Gandalf, a wizard .... BRENT CARVER	Gimli, a Dwarf .... ROSS WILLIAMS
Pippin (Peregrin Took),	Legolas, an Elf .... GABRIEL BURRAFATO
a young hobbit .... OWEN SHARPE	Boromir, a warrior from Gondor .... DION JOHNSTONE
Merry (Meriadoc Brandybuck),	Gollum (Sméagol) .... MICHAEL THERRIAULT
a young hobbit.. DYLAN ROBERTS	Haldir, an Elf of Lothlórien .... FRASER WALTES
Elránien, a wandering Elf .... MONIQUE LUND	Galadriel, Lady of Lothlórien .... REBECCA JACKSON MENDOZA
Saruman, a wizard .... RICHARD McMILLAN	Treebeard, an Ent .... SHAWN WRIGHT
Barliman Butterbur, Landlord of the	Théoden, King of Rohan .... KERRY DOREY
Prancing Pony... SHAWN WRIGHT	Éowyn, Théoden's niece .... AYRIN MACKIE
Bill Ferny, a customer .... PATRICK McMANUS	The Witch King of Angmar .... DON GOUGH
Strider, a Ranger .... EVAN BULIUNG	Gaffer Gamgee, an old hobbit .... SANDERS WHITING

and in order of appearance

Hobbits, Rangers, Wandering Elves, Bree-landers, Black Riders, Elves and Visitors of Rivendell, Orcs, Elves of Lothlórien, Ents,
Soldiers of Rohan, The Army of Allies, Forces of Mordor, People of Gondor

played by

GREG ARMSTRONG-MORRIS, ALEXANDRA BONNET, BRENT BUCHANAN, MATT CASSIDY, MIKE COTA, JOE EIGO,
JOSH EPSTEIN, TROY FELDMAN, MATTHEW GAGNON, NICHOLAS GEDE-LANGE, PETER van GESTEL,
NICO GIANNAKOS, COLIN HEATH, PETER HUCK, CHELINA KENNEDY, BRYCE KULAK, SHANNON LYNCH, TYLER
MURREE, DANNY PATHAN, JESSE ROB, SEAN C. ROBERTSON, VINCENT TONG
Déagol played by JOEL BENSON

SWINGS

OMAR FOREST, KRYSTAL KIRAN GARIB, GRAEME GUTHRIE, COLIN MAIER, PHILLIP NERO, CORY O'BRIEN, LOUISE ST.CYR

Dance and Fight Captain PHILLIP NERO

Assistant Dance Captain JESSE ROBB   Assistant Fight Captain DANNY PATHAN

STAGE MANAGEMENT

Company Manager .... GLENDA FRASER	Assistant Stage Manager.................. MIKE DESCHAMBEAULT
Production Stage Manager .... THE. JOHN GRAY	Assistant Stage Manager.............................. MELANIE KLODT
Stage Manager .... CHRIS PORTER	

ORCHESTRA

Musical Director RICK FOX
Keyboards/Assistant Musical Director FRANKLIN BRASZ, Keyboards JASON JESTADT, Keyboards/Accordion SASHA LUMINSKY,
Violin/Concertmaster MICHELE IRION, Violin/Folk Fiddle/Jouhikko/Nyckelharpa ANNE LINDSAY, Viola JONATHAN CRAIG,
Cello AMY LAING, Bass PATRICK KILBRIDE, Bouzouki LEVON ICHKHANIAN, Flute/Piccolo/Ethnic Flutes LESLIE ALLT,
Trumpet NORMAN ENGEL, French Horn DAVID HASKINS, French Horn DAVID QUACKENBUSH,
Trombone ALASTAIR KAY, Trombone ALISTAIR GASKIN, Bass Trombone TERRY PROMANE,
Percussion PAUL ORMANDY, Percussion NICK COULTER,
Orchestra Contractor JAMES SPRAGG

THE OFFICIAL STAGE COMPANION

CREDITS: LONDON

KEVIN WALLACE and SAUL ZAENTZ
present

Book and Lyrics by SHAUN McKENNA
and MATTHEW WARCHUS

Music by
A.R. RAHMAN
VÄRTTINÄ
with CHRISTOPHER NIGHTINGALE

Set and Costume Designer ROB HOWELL

Lighting Designer PAUL PYANT
Sound Designer SIMON BAKER (for Autograph)
Musical Supervisor CHRISTOPHER NIGHTINGALE
Moving Image Direction by THE GRAY CIRCLE
Literary Consultant LAURIE BATTLE
Special Effects Designer GREGORY MEEH
Illusions and Magic Effects PAUL KIEVE
Musical Director RICHARD BROWN

Associate Costume Designer IRENE BOHAN Associate Set Designer MEGAN HUISH Circus Skills Specialist ALEX FRITH
Associate Lighting Designer DAVID HOWE Associate Sound Designer ALAN LUGGER Fight Director TERRY KING
Casting DAVID GRINDROD ASSOCIATES Associate Choreographer ELLEN KANE Resident Director RUTH CARNEY

Orchestrations by CHRISTOPHER NIGHTINGALE, A.R. RAHMAN and VÄRTTINÄ

Choreographer PETER DARLING

Directed by MATTHEW WARCHUS

THE CAST

In order of speaking

Frodo Baggins, a hobbit	JAMES LOYE	Strider, a Ranger	JÉRÔME PRADON
Bilbo Baggins, a hobbit, Frodo's uncle	TERENCE FRISCH	Bill Ferny, a customer	MICHAEL HOBBS
Gandalf, a wizard	MALCOLM STORRY	Elrond Halfelven, Lord of Rivendell	ANDREW JARVIS
Sam Gamgee, a hobbit, Frodo's gardener	PETER HOWE	Arwen Evenstar, Elrond's daughter	ROSALIE CRAIG
Rosie Cotton, a hobbit	KIRSTY MALPASS	Boromir, a warrior from Gondor	STEVEN MILLER
Pippin (Peregrin Took), a young hobbit	OWEN SHARPE	Gimli, a Dwarf	SÉVAN STEPHAN
Merry (Meriadoc Brandybuck), a young hobbit	RICHARD HENDERS	Legolas, an Elf	MICHAEL ROUSE
Elránien, a wandering Elf	ALEXANDRA BONNET	Gollum (Sméagol)	MICHAEL THERRIAULT
Saruman, a wizard	BRIAN PROTHEROE	Haldir, an Elf of Lothlórien	WAYNE FITZSIMMONS
Barliman Butterbur, Landlord of the Prancing Pony	TIM PARKER	Galadriel, The Lady of Lothlórien	LAURA MICHELLE KELLY
		Treebeard, an Ent	MICHAEL HOBBS
		The Steward of Gondor	TIM MORGAN

and in order of appearance

Hobbits, Rangers, Wandering Elves, Bree-landers, Black Riders, Elves and Visitors of Rivendell, Orcs, Elves of Lothlórien, Ents, The Army of Allies, Forces of Mordor, People of Gondor

played by

GREG BRADLEY, JAMES BYNG, DARREN CARNALL, LEE CLAYDEN, JENNIE DALE, STEPHEN EMERY, BEN EVANS, JOSH FELDSCHUH, ALMA FEROVIC, DAVID GRANT, SHAUN HENSON, CHRISTOPHER D. HUNT, LUKE JOHNSON, STUART NEAL, TIM PARKER, RICHARD ROE, ANDREW ROTHWELL, ROBBIE SCOTCHER, NICK SEARLE, STEVIE TATE-BAUER, JON TSOURAS, GAVIN WILKINSON, KIRK ZAMMIT
Déagol played by DAVID GRANT

SWINGS

CLAIRE DOYLE, CHRIS GAGE, CORRIE MAC, SCOTT OWEN, ADAM SALTER, GLENN WILKINSON, SAM WILMOT

Dance and Fight Captain .... GLENN WILKINSON

Assistant Dance Captain .... RICHARD ROE

STAGE MANAGEMENT

Company Manager	ROGER PENHALE	Assistant Stage Manager	DONALD ROSS
Production Stage Manager	SAM HUNTER	Assistant Stage Manager	JONATHAN HALL
Deputy Stage Manager	ALI WADE	Assistant Stage Manager	SIAN KEMP
Assistant Stage Manager	PETE WAKEMAN		

ORCHESTRA

Musical Director RICHARD BROWN
Keyboard/Assistant Musical Director JEREMY HOLLAND-SMITH, Keyboard LAURIE PERKINS,
Keyboard/Accordion MARCUS TILT, Bazouki/Guitar PETE WALTON, Flutes ANDY FINDON, Violin RICHARD GEORGE,
Violin/Jouhikko CHARLIE BROWN, Viola NICK BARR, Cello JUSTIN PEAERSON, Double Bass LUCY HARE,
Horn RICHARD DILLEY, Horn JONATHAN BAREHAM, Trumpet TOBY COLES, Trombone ADRIAN LANE, Bass Trombone
RICHARD EDWARDS, Percussion JASON HOLLING, Percussion ROB FARRER
Orchestra Manager SYLVIA ADDISON

www.lotr.com

HarperCollins*Publishers*
77–85 Fulham Palace Road,
Hammersmith, London W6 8JB
www.tolkien.co.uk

Published by HarperCollins*Publishers* 2007
1

Mixed Sources
Product group from well-managed
forests and other controlled sources
www.fsc.org Cert no. SW-COC-1806
© 1996 Forest Stewardship Council

FSC